Sounds Like Teen Spirit

Sounds Like Teen Spirit

Stolen Melodies, Ripped-off Riffs, and the Secret History of Rock and Roll

Timothy English

iUniverse, Inc.

New York Lincoln Shanghai

Sounds Like Teen Spirit
Stolen Melodies, Ripped-off Riffs, and the Secret History of Rock and Roll

iUniverse books may be ordered through booksellers or by contacting:

iUniverse
2021 Pine Lake Road, Suite 100
Lincoln, NE 68512
www.iuniverse.com
1-800-Authors (1-800-288-4677)

ISBN-13: 978-0-595-39619-1 (pbk)
ISBN-13: 978-0-595-84021-2 (ebk)
ISBN-10: 0-595-39619-4 (pbk)
ISBN-10: 0-595-84021-3 (ebk)

Printed in the United States of America

3695 41 46 3/08

Contents

Part II   "Not a Second Time?" Beatles Section

Part III   "The Song Remains the Same" Led Zeppelin Section

Part X   Case History Bolton vs. Isley

Part XI   Musical Family Trees

I

"Sounds Like Teen Spirit"

Introduction

This book examines songs that sound like songs that came before them. In dissecting these songs, I hope to shed some light on the nature of creativity and how artists can be influenced by surprisingly diverse sources.

It is not my goal to point fingers and accuse some artists of ripping off others—in most cases the first song was merely a subconscious influence on the writer of the second. Rather, I celebrate all the music mentioned in this book, and I hope you will too.

This book is designed to be an interactive experience. I hope you will seek to compare the various song pairings by listening to each track, and by hearing (or maybe not hearing) the similarities for yourself. I have deliberately sought to include songs that are not overly obscure and may be easily sought out if so desired.

This book includes a diverse collection of artists—from Kraftwerk to Henry Mancini, the Staple Singers to Huey Lewis. It includes songs from as far back as 1928 as well as those released as recently as 2006. All of the original songs were almost certainly known by the writer of the newer song that mimics it. As we shall see, access is a key element of copyright-protection law. A lack of access is the reason many infringement suits are summarily dismissed. If a writer can prove he never heard the work he is accused of copying, he has proven that he could not have plagiarized it. For this reason, most artists have firm policies against listening to songs submitted by aspiring composers. It is rare, yet entirely possible, that two similar works can be composed independent of each other. These no-listening policies help protect prominent musicians from potential lawsuits.

I sought to keep legal technicalities to a merciful minimum, and to instead focus on the music and the artists that created it. As Spinal Tap might say, "It's all about the music, man!"

This book is not concerned with digital sampling of music in creating new music. This practice also reveals an artist's influences. Some artists, like Moby and the Beastie Boys, have used their creativity to compose something new and exciting by sampling old recordings. *Sounds Like Teen Spirit* is concerned with songs and how they came to be created.

As you read this book, you will find that creativity is about being open to diverse influences and creating something that is all your own out of the silence. You will see that great artists possess a willingness to expose themselves to a surprising range of musical styles. As radio becomes more formatted and stations each focus on a single genre of music, new technologies like the Internet, satellite radio, and iPods are giving music lovers the opportunity to program their own listening experiences.

Nothing can illustrate the importance of opening oneself to a wide range of music than listening to the *Beatles Live at the BBC*. Recorded from 1962–65, the album includes many Beatle cover versions of other artists' work. As such it provides a musical genealogical chart of where the Beatles' sound came from. The album includes many Chuck Berry, Carl Perkins, and Little Richard covers as well as Broadway show tunes ("'Til There Was You"), Motown, schmaltzy pop ("The Honeymoon Song"), and even an Ann Margaret cover ("I Just Don't Understand"). John Lennon and Paul McCartney were arguably the greatest composers of the rock era. It would seem that their openness to diverse musical sources, and their ability to incorporate those influences, helped them to create their own innovative sound.

Finally, it is my hope that you will be informed, entertained, and turned on to some great music, possibly for the first time, by reading *Sounds Like Teen Spirit*.

Bill Haley & The Comets's "Rock Around the Clock" (1954)

Sounds Like

Hank Williams's "Move it on Over" (1949)

It is appropriate that this book begin with a song so revolutionary that it kicked off a new era in popular music. Though it was not necessarily the first rock and roll song, "Rock Around the Clock" was the breakthrough song that showed the door to postwar adult pop music. It ushered in the rock era with its R & B influences and teenage fan base. The first song of the rock era was constructed using the same creative musical borrowing that has been a hallmark of rock music ever since.

When Bill Haley & The Comets gathered at New York's famed Pythian Temple studio on the afternoon of Monday, April 12, 1954, few would have supposed that musical history was about to be made. For one thing, the group was there to record their new single, "Thirteen Women (and Only One Man in Town)," a lighthearted look at the aftermath of nuclear holocaust.

Haley was no one's idea of a rock star, a term that had yet to be invented. He was a rotund twenty-eight-year-old from Chester, Pennsylvania.[1] He had started his musical career playing country music but had recently taken up R & B due to the positive reaction it received from audiences at his band's live shows. The band had a nationwide hit in 1953 when "Crazy Man, Crazy" reached No. 12 on the Billboard Hot 100.

Having arrived late to the April 12 recording session, the band had only about forty minutes remaining after they had learned "Thirteen Women" and recorded a usable take. Fortunately they had been playing "Rock Around the Clock" at their club dates for a few months and knew the song well.

Ironically it was two of the players *not* familiar with the song that helped make the recording so memorable. Guitarist Danny Cedrone and drummer Billy Gussak were session players hired for the day's recording. Gussak's distinctive drumming and Cedrone's incredible guitar solo helped turn what might have been a routine recording into one that would change the world.

Surprisingly the song was not a massive hit upon its release the following month. It stalled out at No. 23 on the Billboard chart. It wasn't until the song's inclusion in the movie *Blackboard Jungle* the following year that "Rock Around the Clock" became a phenomenal success. In the meantime, Haley & The Comets had their biggest hit yet with "Shake, Rattle and Roll." The song went to No. 7 on Billboard and stayed on the chart for six months. Several weeks after the recording of "Shake, Rattle and Roll," Cedrone was killed in a fall down a flight of stairs, never to know of the praise his work on "Rock Around the Clock" would receive through the years.

Riding on the popularity of *Blackboard Jungle*, "Rock Around the Clock" hit No. 1 in July 1955 and stayed there for eight weeks. *Blackboard Jungle* was a gritty, low-budget offering about juvenile delinquents challenging adult authority at their Bronx high school. Community and religious leaders denounced the film as immoral and an incitement to violence. Some cities banned the movie or restricted it to adult viewers.

The hard R & B rhythm of "Rock Around the Clock" seemed to add an extra edge of menace to the violence in the movie. Likewise the more "Rock Around the Clock" scared adults in real life, the more kids embraced it.

---

1.   Jim Dawson, *Rock Around the Clock: The Record That Started the Rock Revolution.* (Backbeat Books, 2005).

In fact "Rock Around the Clock" was composed by two middle-aged men—song publisher Jimmy DeKnight, aka James Myers, and songwriter Max C. Freedman. According to author Jim Dawson,[2] Haley simply inserted the music from the verses of one of his favorite songs, Hank Williams's "Move it on Over," into Freedman and DeKnight's composition.

The similarity is obvious to anyone familiar with the two songs.

"Move it on Over" was the first hit—albeit minor—of Williams's painfully brilliant career. George Thoroughgood's 1978 cover version realized the song's full potential as a flat-out rocker.

Williams's recording of "Move it on Over" was a proto rock song that some claim was the first rock and roll record. That's an ongoing debate. But there's no doubt that "Move it on Over" contributed the melody to the song that put rock and roll on the map—Bill Haley & the Comets's "Rock Around the Clock."

---

2.   Ibid.

Ray Parker Jr.'s "Ghostbusters" (1984)

Sounds Like

Huey Lewis & the News's "I Want a New Drug" (1983)

Back in 1984, Huey Lewis freaked out[3] the first time he heard Ray Parker Jr.'s "Ghostbusters" on the radio. Was he upset that a song this trite was on its way to No. 1 for three weeks? No, he was upset that Parker had stolen his song "I Want a New Drug," a No. 8 hit the previous year.

Indeed, the songs had a lot in common. The groove and verses were remarkably similar. Moreover Columbia Pictures had approached Lewis about contributing a song for the movie *Ghostbusters*, but Lewis had declined. It was reported that the film producers had asked Parker to come up with a song that was "simple and easy" and included the word *Ghostbusters*. Lewis's "I Want a New Drug" was reportedly played for Parker to give him an exact idea of what the producers were after.

Lewis & the News brought a five-million-dollar lawsuit against Parker, Columbia, and director Ivan Reitman, claiming copyright infringement. It

---

3.   VH1 *Behind the Music*, Episode 144. Originally Broadcast March, 2001.

appeared that Lewis had strong documented evidence on his side, and the case was settled out of court in 1984.

In 2001, Lewis told VH1's *Behind the Music*,[4] "The offensive part was not that Ray Parker Jr. had ripped the song off. It was symbolic of an industry that wants something…they wanted to buy it. We were adamant that it wasn't for sale. In the end, I suppose they were right. I suppose it was for sale because basically they bought it!"

After the program aired, Parker brought suit against Lewis, claiming he had violated a confidentiality agreement negotiated as a part of the original lawsuit settlement.

The movie *Ghostbusters* broke box-office records as the highest-grossing comedy ever released. The following year, Lewis & the News had a much better experience with Hollywood movie making when their song "The Power of Love" went to No. 1 after its inclusion in the film, *Back to the Future*.

---

4.   Ibid.

Tom Petty & The Heartbreakers's "Breakdown" (1977)

Sounds Like

The Animals's "Cheating" (1966)

While a lot of ink has been spilled praising the long and prolific careers of Neil Young and Bruce Springsteen, perhaps it's time that Tom Petty receive his due. Think about what makes up his thirty-year career: great songwriting, dynamic live shows, a great backing band in the Heartbreakers (guitarist Mike Campbell is surely one of rock and roll's most underrated players), a stint with the Traveling Wilburys, and consistently strong albums, each of which features at least one song you'll love. Not only that, in 1981 he successfully fought his record company, MCA Records, to keep it from raising the retail price of his *Hard Promises* album to the then-unheard-of sum of $8.98.

Petty's music has always worn its mid-1960s Byrds and British Invasion influences on its sleeve. "Breakdown" was Petty's first hit record, reaching No. 40 on the Billboard chart in the fall of 1977. The verses of "Breakdown" are musically very similar to the verses in "Cheating," an obscure Animals's song—at least to the general public.

"Cheating" was the B-side of "Don't Bring Me Down," a No. 12 hit for the Animals. Both songs appeared on the album *Animalization* in the United States. It can be assumed that Petty & the Heartbreakers were familiar with

"Cheating" because, in the beginning of their careers, they often played "Don't Bring Me Down" in concert. A live version of "Don't Bring Me Down" is included on Petty's 1986 album *Pack Up the Plantation: Live!* Another old Animals's track, "I'm Cryin'," has also been a regular feature at Petty's concerts.

Petty has been forthright about the obvious influence of the Animals on his music.[5] His talent has afforded him the opportunity to play and create with musical heroes like George Harrison, Bob Dylan, and Roy Orbison, while helping revive the careers of Roger McGuinn and Del Shannon. I'd say that makes him a true rock and roll hero.

---

5.   Paul Zollo, *Conversations With Tom Petty.* (London: Omnibus, 2005), 19.

Steely Dan's "Rikki, Don't Lose That Number" (1974)

Sounds Like

Horace Silver's "Song for My Father" (1964)

You've never heard of Horace Silver? Steely Dan's Donald Fagan and Walter Becker sure have. Silver is one of jazz's greatest composers and pianists, specializing in the "hard bop" style he helped pioneer as a member of Art Blakey's Jazz Messengers in the 1950s. "Song for My Father" is the title track of his most popular album. It features trumpeter Carmel Jones and stellar tenor sax man Joe Henderson, and it stands as one of the truly great albums in jazz history.

In "Rikki, Don't Lose That Number," Steely Dan lifts the bass pattern that is repeated in variations throughout "Song for My Father." While it's true that this pattern was close to the basic bossa nova beat popular in jazz in the early '60s, the grooves of the two songs sound very much alike.

Steely Dan's quirkily melodic compositions of the 1970s incorporated jazz music more successfully than any other group working in the rock idiom. Many prominent jazz players recorded with the band as part of a diverse and ever-changing group of studio session man. Steely Dan's impeccably produced music has aged well, and still sounds fresh after thirty years.

"Rikki, Don't Lose That Number" can be found on Steely Dan's third album, 1974's *Pretzel Logic*. The single rose to No. 4 on the charts and proved to be the biggest pop hit of the band's career. "The Dan" reunited in 2000 and released *Two Against Nature*, a return to form that won the Grammy for Album of the Year. They followed up with *Everything Must Go* in 2003.

In 1999 Blue Note rereleased a digitally remastered "Song for my Father" with bonus tracks. Both that CD and the original album feature a photo of Silver's father. Silver continues to perform.

The Doors's "Hello, I Love You" (1968)

Sounds Like

The Kinks's "All Day and All of the Night" (1964)

These are two of the most popular and enduring recordings of the 1960s, and they share a remarkably similar melody line.

The Kinks's song is a gloriously raucous riff-based rocker, very much in the style of their first hit, "You Really Got Me." It was written by Kinks's leader Ray Davies, surely one of rock's most underrated songwriters. The exciting guitar solo is rumored to have been performed by none other than Jimmy Page, then a London session man.

The "hook" of "Hello, I Love You" is a slight rephrasing of the verse opening and chorus of "All Day and All of the Night." This phrase forms the basis of the two songs and is repeated many times in both. That said, one can listen to "Hello, I Love You" without immediately harkening back to "All Day and All of the Night." This is due to the very different rhythm and guitar pattern featured on "Hello, I Love You."

"Hello, I Love You" was at least three years old when it was recorded for the Doors's third album, *Waiting for the Sun*.[6] Having recorded two albums in the span of one year, the band apparently had a few new songs to record. "Hello, I Love You" is credited to all four band members and incorporates Morrison's colorful, poetic imagery to great effect.

"Hello, I Love You" held the No. 1 spot on Billboard for two weeks and was the biggest hit of the Doors's career, with the exception of "Light My Fire" in 1967.

In his autobiography, Ray's brother, Kinks's guitarist Dave Davies wrote, "'Hello, I Love You' was obviously plagiarized from 'All Day and All of the Night.'"[7] He went on to state that the songs share the same chord structure, the same rhythm, and their choruses share the same melody. Dave claims Ray turned down their lawyer's advice to sue the Doors saying it wasn't worth the trouble.

In 2003 Doors's drummer John Densmore brought suit to block ex-bandmates Ray Manzarek and Robbie Kreiger from touring under the Doors name with ex-Cult singer Ian Astbury standing in for Jim Morrison. Ray Davies issued *Other People's Lives* to critical acclaim in 2006. It is his first solo album.

---

6. The 1965 version of "Hello, I Love You" was released on The Door's *Box Set* in 1997.
7. Dave Davies, *Kink: An Autobiography* (New York: Hyperion, 1996).

The J. Geils Band's "Love Stinks" (1980)

Sounds Like

The Troggs's "Wild Thing" (1966)

The crunching guitar riff that opens and propels "Wild Thing" is surely one of the mightiest and most memorable in rock. Troggs's lead singer Reg Presley delivered the song in a leering manner that perfectly matched its powerful chorus. It mattered little that the riff was a "Louie Louie" lift, and the lyrics...well, let's just say that Bob Dylan had nothing to worry about. Even so, "Wild Thing" is one of the greatest songs in rock history.

In 1980 The J. Geils Band was continuing to evolve toward a more mainstream sound, building on the R & B it was known for early in its career. "Love Stinks" is the title track from the album the band released that year, and the single reached the Top 40. Its similarity to "Wild Thing" is immediately apparent in the guitar chord progression that opens the song. Guitarist J. Geils plays a distorted and slowed-down version of "Wild Thing's" opening. This progression repeats in the chorus (as it does in "Wild Thing") where it is punctuated by lead singer Peter Wolf's exclamation that "Love Stinks"—two notes that echo Presley's two-note "Wild Thing" shout.

The J. Geils Band enjoyed its greatest commercial success in 1981 with its *Centerfold* album. The title track was No. 1 for six weeks. Then Wolf split from the band to go on to a less-than-spectacular solo career. The band was not the same without him. Wolf returned to the fold for a tour in 1999.

Bruce Springsteen spent a stretch during the early '70s performing as an opening act for the J. Geils Band. Following that partnership, Wolf was often cited as having influenced Springsteen's onstage persona. In recent years, Wolf has been an occasional guest at Springsteen shows, most recently at the Boston stop on Springsteen's 2006 *Seeger Sessions* tour.

Fun fact: In 1967 a Robert F. Kennedy impersonator going by the name "Senator Bobby" had a Top 40 hit with a novelty version of "Wild Thing." Chip Taylor, the author of "Wild Thing," was the man behind this bizarre bit of pop history.

Tommy Page's "I'll Be Your Everything" (1990)

Sounds Like

Percy Sledge's "I'll Be Your Everything" (1974)

Tommy Page was a protégé of New Kids on the Block mastermind Maurice Starr. Page wrote his song "I'll Be Your Everything" with Jordan Knight and Danny Wood of New Kids.

This faux-soul confection actually topped the Billboard chart in the spring of 1990. At the time, New Kids On the Block was at the height of their popularity with the teenybopper set. Released in 1988, their *Hangin' Tough* album sold eight million copies.

The problem was that the 1990 recording of "I'll Be Your Everything" shared both its title and some of its music with a somewhat obscure sixteen-year-old Percy Sledge song. Knight, Wood and Page soon found themselves in court, having been sued for copyright infringement by Northside Partners, owners of the Sledge song.

Percy Sledge is best known for his immortal 1966 hit, "When a Man Loves a Woman," but he also recorded lesser known classics, including "Take Time to Know Her" and "It Tears Me Up." The fact that his recording of George

Soule's "I'll Be Your Everything" rose to only No. 62 on Billboard's Hot 100 allowed lawyers for Knight, Page and Wood to credibly claim that the trio had never heard the song. In addition they sought to show that the songs differed musically, with Knight taking to the keyboard to show how he created his song (and providing a thrill for New Kids's fans attending the trial to support their heroes).

Lawyers for the plaintiffs argued that the defendants could have heard Sledge's song during oldies listening sessions with Starr. Starr played bass on Page's song, and the plaintiffs sought to show that Starr's bass playing made the song sound similar to Sledge's recording. Certainly Starr was more likely to be familiar with Sledge's song than the trio of young writers. Starr was a young adult in 1974 when the record was on the charts, the same year the song reached No. 15 on Billboard's soul chart.

Listening to the songs back-to-back reveals that they have entirely different verses. The choruses are similar, but are not exactly the same; the songs share the same tempo; and there is identical title repetition in the chorus.

In addition to the defendants, the June 1992 trial in New York heard testimony from Sledge, Starr, Soule, and various musicologists. Defense lawyers sought to use the fact that the songs shared a title to their advantage by arguing that it would have been foolhardy to use the same lyrics if you were stealing the music from a song. The judge reminded jurors that copyright laws do not protect song titles.

The jury found that the defendants had not infringed on Northside's copyright.[8] The fact that Knight, Page and Wood could plausibly claim to have never heard the 1974 song greatly helped their case.

The advent of grunge in 1991 brought a quick end to the popularity of the New Kids's brand of pretty-boy pop. Or did it? By 1998 Kurt Cobain was long dead and the pop charts were ruled by the likes of *NSYNC and the Backstreet Boys, groups that were obviously following the old New Kids's formula for success. Pop star Britney Spears and *NSYNC's Justin Timberlake seem to have learned from the New Kids's experience that it is necessary to broaden their appeal to older audiences.

In 1999 comeback albums were released by former New Kids on the Block members Knight and Joe McIntyre. In 2004 Knight made a comeback of sorts

8. Fred Kirby, "New Kids Acquitted on Copyright Charges," *Billboard Magazine*, June 27, 1992.

appearing with B-grade celebrities on VH1's the *Surreal Life*. Perhaps Knight will pen a tune for Page and rescue him from obscurity. "When a Man Loves a Woman" anyone?

R.E.M.'s "Hope" (1998)

Sounds Like

Leonard Cohen's "Suzanne" (1968)

"Hope" is more reminiscent of "Suzanne" lyrically than musically. But as fans of Leonard Cohen, R.E.M. decided to give Cohen a songwriting credit on "Hope," rather than risk legal action.

Cohen is one of the more enigmatic figures in pop music. Born in Montreal in 1934, Cohen was well into his thirties by the time his debut album, *Songs of Leonard Cohen*, was released in 1968. "Suzanne" was released as a single from the album, but failed to chart in the United States. The album itself made it only to No. 83 in the United States, but fared better in the UK where it got to No. 13.

By 1968 Cohen had already published the novel, *Beautiful Losers*, as well as several volumes of poetry with catchy titles like *Flowers of Hitler* and *Parasites of Heaven*. The latter volume was published in 1966 and contained the poem that evolved into "Suzanne."

Cohen didn't sing his songs as much as he recited them. Like many of his songs, "Suzanne" has a ruminative, sad feeling, evoking lost loves and rainy afternoons. Not surprisingly, this same feel pervades *Up*, R.E.M.'s first album following the retirement of drummer Bill Berry. *Up* consists of slow, dream-like songs, such as "Nightsleeper" and "Hope." (The song that precedes "Hope" on *Up* is "Suspicion," which has a melody that sounds like "Laughing" by the Guess Who.) This move away from their traditional sound marked a new direction for the band and received a mixed reaction from fans and critics.

In 1991 R.E.M. contributed a cover of "First We Take Manhattan" for the Cohen tribute album *I'm Your Fan*. Another Cohen tribute, *Tower of Song*, was released in 1995. It contained Cohen songs covered by the likes of Elton John, Billy Joel, and Bono.

Cohen moved to a California Zen Buddhist center in 1993. He arose at 3 AM and lived in an area no larger than a cut-rate motel room. He left the monastery in the late '90s and has recently become involved in a lawsuit against his former business manager. Cohen claims he was robbed of most of his life savings.

AND FURTHERMORE...Have you ever noticed that R.E.M.'s "How the West Was Won and Where it Got Us" sounds an awful lot like (of all things) Pink Floyd's "Learning to Fly"?

Me too!

The Grass Roots's "Let's Live for Today" (1967)

Sounds Like

The Drifters's "I Count the Tears" (1960)

Both the Grass Roots's "Let's Live for Today" and the Drifters's "I count the Tears" are fine songs that stand on their own terms. Though they are performed in different styles, a casual listener will note the musical similarities of their respective choruses. "Let's Live for Today" is a direct descendent of "I Count the Tears" with the breeding ground being that hotbed of rock and roll...Italy?

Yes, Italy. In 1965 a band called the Rokes rewrote "I Count the Tears" as "Piangi Con Me" ("Cry With Me") and had a big hit in Italy. In 1967 the Grass Roots rewrote "Piangi" as "Let's Live for Today" and had a No. 8 hit in the United States.

The choruses of "I Count the Tears" and "Let's Live for Today" are identical, right down to the "na-na's" of the former and the "la-la's" of the latter.

Legendary New York songwriting team Doc Pomus and Mort Shuman wrote "I Count the Tears." They authored a number of classic songs, including "This Magic Moment," "Little Sister," and "Save the Last Dance for

23

Me,"—a song John Lennon thought Paul McCartney re-wrote to come up with the melody to "Hey Jude."

Roseanne Cash did a nice version of "I Count the Tears" on a 1993 Pomus tribute album, *Till the Night is Gone.*

Steve Winwood's "Roll With It" (1988)

Sounds Like

Junior Walker & the All-Stars's "I'm a Roadrunner" (1965)

Steve Winwood and songwriting partner Will Jennings set out to write a tribute to Motown sound and succeeded in turning out a No. 1 hit. However the writers of "Roadrunner," the legendary Motown team of Holland-Dozier-Holland, thought "Roll With It" was more an imitation of their song than a tribute to Motown. In 1990 The writing team brought suit against Winwood and Jennings, claiming plagiarism.[9]

Winwood was a big Junior Walker fan. He once stated that he "based the original Traffic on Jr. Walker and the All-Stars." He met his wife, Eugenia, at a Walker show in New York in the 1980s.

"Roll With It" attempts to update the Motown sound for the late '80s. It uses a beat and instrumentation similar to those on "Roadrunner." Where Winwood and Jennings really got themselves in trouble was in the chorus

---

9.   UPI, "Suit asserts Winwood Hit was Stolen." *The Los Angeles Times*, November 20, 1990.

where the words "Roll with it, baby" sound like Walker's "I'm a roadrunner, baby." This similarity must have made it crystal clear that the inspiration for "Roll With It" was "I'm a Roadrunner."

Rod Stewart was able to pull off this Motown pastiche trick to better effect with his 1991 hit "The Motown Song." "The Motown Song" sounds more than a little like the Temptations "The Girl's Alright with Me," but that's OK, because none other than the Temptations themselves backed Stewart up on the song.

"Roll With It" provided Winwood with the biggest hit of his career, with both the song and the album going to No. 1 on Billboard charts in 1988. He has yet to hit the Top 40 in the years since. On the other hand, Jennings has gone on to even greater success as the co-author of "Tears in Heaven" with Eric Clapton. He also co-authored the monster hit "My Heart Will Go On" (sung by Celine Dion), with *Titanic* composer James Horner.

As for the lawsuit, it was settled out of court. The music publishing royalty organization, Broadcast Music International (BMI), today lists the authors of "Roll With It" as Jennings-Winwood-Holland-Dozier-Holland.[10] When Jennings and Winwood set out to "pay" tribute, this probably wasn't what they had in mind.

---

10. See Internet site www.bmi.com.

Phil Collins's "Sussudio" (1984)

Sounds Like

Prince's "1999" (1983)

Few artists have dominated the pop charts the way Prince did in 1984. His *Purple Rain* soundtrack album produced three No. 1 singles: "When Doves Cry," "Let's Go Crazy," and the title song, "Purple Rain." The album eventually sold more than ten million copies in the United States alone. Likewise the movie *Purple Rain* was enormously successful, grossing seventy million dollars (more than ten times the film's cost) and going on to become the tenth largest-grossing film of the year. In addition cover versions of three of Prince's compositions became top-ten hits: Chaka Khan's "I Feel for You," Sheena Easton's "Sugar Walls," and Prince protégé Sheila E's "The Glamorous Life." Prince exerted a multi-faceted dominance of 1984's pop scene, similar to what the Beatles and the Bee Gees accomplished in 1964 and 1978 respectively.

Prince broke through to a mass audience the previous year with the song, "Little Red Corvette," from the album *1999*. The song "1999" received wide airplay and reached No. 12 on the charts during the summer of 1983.

The overall sound and production of Phil Collins's "Sussudio" sounds incredibly like "1999," a fact that, at the time, was often pointed out by DJs. The synthesizer riff that prevails throughout "Sussudio" is but a minor variation of the riff played on "1999." Not being a dummy, Collins kept this one out of lawsuit territory by supplying an original melody. In responding to criticism that he had ripped off "1999," Collins said, "I'm a big Prince fan…I loved that song. I bought it when it first came out, and I used to listen to it on the road. I took the tempo (of '1999')…I locked it in the drum machine. That was the end of it…'Sussudio' was actually changed once because it was starting to sound a bit *too* much like Prince."[11]

The public liked "Sussudio," and the song went to No. 1 after being released as a single in the spring of 1985. This gave Collins three No. 1 solo singles in a row, a feat accomplished by only three other male vocalists: Elvis Presley, Michael Jackson, and Andy Gibb. "Sussudio" is on Collins's album, *No Jacket Required*, which went on to win the 1985 Grammy Award for Album of the Year. Interestingly the next Collins release, "Don't Lose My Number," bore a passing lyrical similarity to Steely Dan's "Rikki, Don't Lose That Number."

---

11.   Fred Bronson. *The Billboard Book of Number One Hits.* (New York: Billboard. 1988).

The Cure's "Love Song" (1989)

Sounds Like

The Church's "Under the Milky Way" (1988)

The similarities of these two songs might not seem apparent at first, but closer examination reveals "Love Song" to be a rewrite of "Under the Milky Way," a Top 40 hit from the previous year. The distinctive chord pattern in the verses of each song—played on acoustic guitars on "Milky Way" and synthesizers on "Love Song"—are strikingly similar. After the verses, each song speeds up and modulates before returning to the opening pattern.

"Under the Milky Way" is a haunting and ethereal song that provided the Church with its biggest hit. The song is on their excellent *Starfish* album. After a couple more albums were released in the early '90s, the band seemed to fall off the edge of the world. They *were* from Australia; maybe they just went home. In actuality they have continued to record with less commercial success. In 2006 their CD *Uninvited, Like the Clouds* was released to positive reviews.

"Love Song" was written by Cure leader Robert Smith as a wedding present for his wife, Mary.[12] The lyrics expressed a sentimentality not usually

---

12. Dave Thomson. *In Between Days: An Armchair Guide to the Cure.* (London: Helter Skelter, 2005).

found in Cure songs. "Love Song" was the biggest chart hit of the Cure's career, rising to No. 2 on the Billboard singles chart. It was ably assisted by a video that saw heavy rotation on MTV. Since then only 1992's "Friday I'm in Love" has cracked the Top 40. The Cure returned with a self-titled new album in 2004. Many fans welcomed the effort as a return to form for Smith and the Cure.

The Beach Boys's "Surfin' U.S.A." (1963)

Sounds Like

Chuck Berry's "Sweet Little Sixteen" (1958)

In early 1963, the Beach Boys were enjoying breakthrough success in a career that would span decades. Although they had a top-twenty hit the previous fall with "Surfin' Safari," "Surfin' U.S.A." was their first top-five hit and their first million-seller. The song epitomized the sunny good spirits with which the Beach Boys's music became synonymous.

In contrast, things were going less than swimmingly for Chuck Berry as 1962 turned into 1963. In fact he was incarcerated in a federal prison in Leavenworth, Kansas. He was halfway through serving a twenty-month sentence for violating the Mann Act, which prohibited transporting women over state lines for the purpose of prostitution.

It was apparent to anyone familiar with the two songs that "Surfin' U.S.A." was Berry's "Sweet Little Sixteen" with a new set of lyrics that substituted surfing towns for the U.S. cities in Berry's song. In addition "Surfin' U.S.A" author Brian Wilson added an urgent 4/4 drumbeat to the verses, sped up the chorus, and added harmony vocals—"Inside outside U.S.A."—that gave the song a different character than Berry's original.

Berry's record label, Chess, was not known for being overly generous with its artists. (Remember the story the Stones told of seeing Muddy Waters painting the ceiling of Chess studio during their 1964 visit?) In this case, Chess apparently did right by Berry. ARC Music, the Chess Bros. music publishing company, pointed out the similarities in the songs to Wilson's publisher. Marshall Chess later recalled, "It was total infringement. Had Brian Wilson's lawyers come to Chuck and said 'We're doing this with our lyrics; let's go 50/50 on the copyright,' it probably wouldn't have happened. But Brian Wilson tried to steal the song, so it became a copyright infringement...Chuck became the full writer."[13]

Subsequent releases of "Surfin' U.S.A." list the song's writer as Chuck Berry. This decision appears to have been made by the notorious Murray Wilson, Brian's father, who was the administrator of Brian's publishing company, Sea of Tunes. In more recent years, the credit has been changed to Brian Wilson/Chuck Berry, a more accurate description of the authorship of the song.

In a radio interview about the genesis of "Surfin' U.S.A.," Wilson said, "I was going with a girl named Judy...and her brother Jimmy was this surfer. He knew all the surfing spots. I started humming the melody to 'Sweet Little Sixteen' and I got fascinated with the fact of doing it. I thought to myself 'God! What about trying to put surf lyrics to 'Sweet Little Sixteen's'" melody?' The concept was about they're doing this in this city, and they're doing that in that city. So I said to Jimmy...'I want to do a song mentioning all the surf spots.' So he gave me a list."[14]

Asked by *Guitar Player* magazine if he enjoyed the cover versions of his songs by other artists Berry replied, "Every one of them. Excepting the first one I heard. The Beach Boys did 'Sweet Little Sixteen' and it was called ('Surfin' U.S.A.'). Well, that's no compliment. They named it different. But BMI noticed it, and here come the royalties. So it doesn't really matter."[15]

---

13. Bruce Pegg. *Brown Eyed Handsome Man: The Life and Hard Times of Chuck Berry*. (New York: Taylor and Francis, 2002).

14. Keith Badman. *The Beach Boys: The Definitive Diary of America's Greatest Band*. (San Francisco: Backbeat Books, 2004), 32.

15. Editors of Goldmine Magazine. *Roots of Rock Digest*. (Iola, WI: Krause Publications, 1999).

Berry's hurt feelings have no doubt been assuaged by the fact that "Surfin' U.S.A." has been released on numerous Beach Boys anthologies in the forty years since its release. To paraphrase Liberace, Berry has been crying all the way to the bank. The song even briefly reentered the Top 40 in 1974, when the Beach Boys's popularity was revived with their *Endless Summer* compilation.

In 1976 the Beach Boys returned to the charts for the first time in years with a cover of Berry's "Rock and Roll Music." It was their biggest hit since "Good Vibrations" ten years earlier.

Few major artists from the 1960s have seen their reputations elevated in the ensuing years as much as Brian Wilson. This can be attributed to the timeless quality of his music, as well as to the fact that his music is no longer tied to the less-than-hip image the Beach Boys projected in the '60s.

In 2004 Wilson released *Smile*, a new recording of songs from the Beach Boys's legendary "lost" album from 1967. Although many of the songs had seen the light of day on various Beach Boys releases through the years, this was the first time the album was heard as a whole. Considering that the frustrations associated with the original project may have helped to facilitate his breakdown, finishing the album almost forty years later was a profound act of personal courage and perseverance. The music wasn't bad either.

It's ironic that while the Beach Boys will forever be remembered for Brian's brilliant melodies, the song that put them on the map had Brian's words set to someone else's melody.

John Cougar Mellencamp's "Small Town" (1985)

Sounds Like

Ian Hunter's "When the Daylight Comes" (1979)

Considering the fact that Ian Hunter's album *You're Never Alone with a Schizophrenic* was so widely heard on FM radio upon its release, the absence of songs like "Cleveland Rocks," "Just Another Night," and "When the Daylight Comes" from today's airwaves is indeed curious. Perhaps these songs were never entered into the computer that tells the programmers of classic-rock stations what to play. Is there anyone out there who needs to hear "Baba O'Reilly" again in this lifetime?

After leaving Mott the Hoople in 1974, Hunter launched a solo career with assistance from former-David Bowie guitarist Mick Ronson. *Schizophrenic* was the most successful album of Hunter's career. Its songs formed the core of his follow-up live album, *Welcome to the Club*, released in 1980.

Backing up Hunter and Ronson on *Schizophrenic* were members of Bruce Springsteen's E Street Band, including drummer Max Weinberg, pianist Roy Bittan, and bassist Gary Tallent. The Springsteen-like backing suited Hunter's music well and gave the record the radio-friendly sound of the time.

Indeed most of these same E Street band members had just finished backing up Meatloaf on his multi-platinum *Bat Out of Hell* album.

Listening to Mellencamp's "Small Town" suggests that one man listening to Hunter's album was John Cougar Mellencamp. The two songs share the exact same chord pattern—a pattern so prominent in "Small Town" that it, in effect, serves as the song's chorus. Hunter adds a middle eight musical section to break the monotony, while Cougar Mellencamp does not. To be fair, the songs' melodies are not similar, though they compete for attention with the chordal riff in both songs.

"Small Town" is on Cougar Mellencamp's excellent *Scarecrow* album and reached the No. 6 spot on the Billboard singles chart.

Hunter turned sixty-seven in 2006 and is still actively touring, although it appears he's past his prime as far as album sales go. Sadly Ronson, his collaborator and friend, passed away in 1994.

......AND FURTHERMORE. Another *Scarecrow* track, "R.O.C.K. In the U.S.A." bares more than a passing resemblance to the Romantics 1980 hit "What I Like About You."

Bruce Springsteen's "Pink Cadillac" (1984)

Sounds Like

Henry Mancini's "Theme From Peter Gunn" (1959)

"Theme From Peter Gunn's" creeping guitar and snarling horns immediately bring to mind noirish images of bad guys on the wrong side of town. It provided the theme to *Peter Gunn,* the TV detective show that ran from 1958–1961. Mancini's jazzy score was considered highly innovative for its time, and is today far better remembered than the show itself.

What Bruce Springsteen seeks to do in "Pink Cadillac" is to borrow this menacing theme as a platform on which to construct his song. Thus the song lifts "Peter Gunn's" low E-string guitar pattern, and Clarence Clemons's[16] sax mimics Mancini's horn section. Springsteen did not deem "Pink Cadillac" worthy of inclusion on his *Born in the USA* album and instead released it as the

---

16. Clemons recorded "Theme from Peter Gunn" for the *Porky's Revenge* soundtrack, issued in 1985. One of the better rock soundtrack albums, it featured songs by Dave Edmunds, Jeff Beck, and George Harrison's excellent version of the obscure Dylan song "I Don't Want to Do It."

B-side (remember B-sides?) of his "Dancing in the Dark" single. It proved a favorite of fans, and was preceded in concert by a story about temptation in which Bruce raved like a preacher.

In addition to arranging and conducting, Mancini composed the music for hundreds of movies. He was a four-time Oscar winner and a twenty-time Grammy winner. Among his most noteworthy compositions are the beautiful "Moon River," from *Breakfast at Tiffany's,* with lyrics by Johnny Mercer; "The Pink Panther Theme"; and "Theme from *Love Story.*"

When airing TV retrospectives about the eventful summer of 1969—the summer of Woodstock, Manson, Chappaquiddick, and the moon landing—how often is it recalled that Mancini's "Love Theme from *Romeo and Juliet*" held the top spot in Billboard for two weeks that summer? Such nuances of life don't always fit into the shaping of our collective memory.

Mancini passed away in 1994, just as the terminally-hip crowd began to rediscover his music as part of the lounge revival. "Love Theme from *Romeo and Juliet*" has become a favorite piece for female ice skaters to perform to, and was heard by millions viewing the 2006 Winter Olympics in Turin, Italy.

David Bowie's "Changes" (1971)

Sounds Like

The Pretty Things's "Tripping" (1967)

If American rock music fans have ever heard of the Pretty Things, it may be because guitarist Dick Taylor was almost a Rolling Stone. He used to play with Jagger, Richards, and Brian Jones back in 1961–62 as the Stones were forming. The Pretty Things had a string of successful singles in Britain in the mid '60s, but failed to achieve a breakthrough Stateside. They began a shift from straight R & B toward psychedelia on their 1967 album *Emotions*, which includes "Tripping." In 1968 they released *S.F. Sorrow*, which was the first "rock opera," and served as an influence on the creation of the Who's *Tommy*, released the following year.

One listen to "Tripping" will immediately bring to mind David Bowie's "Changes" because the word *"tripping"* and the word *"changes"* are intentionally stuttered in both songs. The Who's Roger Daltrey memorably stuttered through "My Generation" in order to underline the confusion of the song's narrator. Although this device might seem incidental when used in "Changes," it is actually an integral part of the song. It is used each time the word is sung, distinctively planting the song's title in the memory of the listener.

"Changes" is on Bowie's 1971 album *Hunky Dory*, which established him as a major star in the United States. The song has been an FM radio staple since its release. Appropriately enough, the song that follows "Changes" on the album is "Oh! You Pretty Things"—a song not ostensibly about the band.

Bowie displayed his respect for the Pretty Things's music when he recorded two of their songs, "Don't Bring Me Down" and "Rosalyn," on his 1973 album of cover songs, *Pin-Ups*.

In 1999, the Pretty Things had a mini revival as they released a new album and re-released their old albums on CD, including *Emotions*. In the fall of 1999, Bowie released the back-to-basics album *Hours*, which featured "The Pretty Things Are Going to Hell." Wait a minute, David, it was you who nicked their song, not the other way around.

Joe Jackson's "Breaking Us in Two" (1982)

Sounds Like

Badfinger's "Day After Day" (1971)

The first line of "Breaking Us in Two" is remarkably similar to the music at the beginning of "Day After Day." Jackson has wisely added a jazzy chord in the middle of the phase and some more notes at the end. These opening musical phrases are then repeated in both songs, making "Breaking Us in Two" extremely reminiscent of the Badfinger song.

If any of you parents ever wish to dissuade a child from going into the music business, you may want to tell them Badfinger's sad saga.[17] Badfinger was signed to the Beatles's Apple label and became the Fab Four's protégé. Paul McCartney wrote and produced the band's first hit, "Come and Get It." George Harrison produced "Day After Day," and contributed its distinctive slide guitar break. But Badfinger's career was ruined by poor business deci-

---

17. Mojo, VH1 *Behind the Music: Badfinger.* Originally Broadcast November, 2000. Additional info. see DuNoyer, Paul. April 1998. *"A Hard Day's Night."* Mojo, 40–51.

sions and a manager they accused of stealing money from their publishing escrow account. This resulted in the band's 1974 album, *Wish You Were Here*, being recalled by Warner Brothers only weeks after its release.

These hassles proved too much for Pete Ham, Badfinger's singer, guitarist, and the author of "Day After Day." He hung himself in his garage on April 23, 1975. The band broke up after Ham's suicide. In the late '70s, bassist Joey Molland and guitarist Tom Evans reformed Badfinger and released two albums, neither of which sold well. Despondent over this and continuing hassles that prevented him from receiving royalty payments, Evans killed himself on November 23, 1983. He hung himself from a tree in his backyard.

The 1990s saw the Ham-Evans song "Without You," a Badfinger album track that was taken to No. 1 by Harry Nilsson in 1972, become a top-five hit for Mariah Carey. Many of the old Badfinger business disputes were resolved, but it was too late to help Pete Ham or Tom Evans.

Two excellent compilations of Pete Ham's demos, *Golder's Green* and *7 Park Ave.*, have been released in recent years. In 2005 drummer Mike Gibbins died, and 1971's *Concert for Bangladesh was released.* The concert features Badfinger supplying back-up for the event's all-star lineup.

Jon Bon Jovi's "Billy, Get Your Guns" (1990)

Sounds Like

Billy Joel's "That's Not Her Style" (1989)

Jon Bon Jovi's "Billy, Get Your Guns" and Billy Joel's "That's Not Her Style" have choruses that are nearly identical musically. Joel's song is a clunky rocker apparently written for his then wife, Christie Brinkley. Bon Jovi's song is a hard-driving number and boasts Jeff Beck and Elton John as session players. Because "That's Not Her Style" was widely heard on the radio in late 1989, might we speculate that it influenced the writing of "Billy, Get Your Guns"?

"That's Not Her Style" was not a hit single, but it was included on Joel's highly successful *Storm Front* album. "Billy, Get Your Guns" was on Bon Jovi's soundtrack to the less-than-memorable movie *Young Guns II*, which also included his No. 1 hit, "Blaze of Glory." The movie marked a turning point for Bon Jovi in that he appeared on screen in a bit part. He has since acted in several Hollywood features and seems to have a promising career as a film actor. In 2002 he acted in a recurring role in the TV show *Ally McBeal*.

Joel returned to the concert stage in 2006, after a "retirement" of several years.

By the way, did I mention that "Billy, Get your Guns" is actually a pretty good song?

Bon Jovi's "You Give Love a Bad Name" (1986)

Sounds Like

Bonnie Tyler's "If You Were A Woman (and I Was a Man)" (1986)

Speaking of Bon Jovi…

Play Bon Jovi's "You Give Love a Bad Name" and Bonnie Tyler's "If You Were A Woman (and I Was a Man)" back-to-back and be shocked at how incredibly alike they are. They share a cappella intros, note-for-note choruses, and similar rhythms. Read the songwriting credits for the songs and the shock ends. The same man had a hand in writing both songs.

That man is Desmond Child, the sole writer of "If You Were a Woman (and I was a Man)," and the co-author of "You Give Love a Bad Name," along with Jon Bon Jovi and guitarist Richie Sambora. Child went on to collaborate with the band on such smashes as "Livin' on a Prayer," "Keep the Faith," and "Bad Medicine." He also co-wrote "Dude (Looks Like a Lady) for Aerosmith. On the other side of the ledger, Child also gave the world Ricky Martin's "Livin' La Vida Loca" and Siquo's immortal "Thong Song."

Tyler has sometimes been described as "the female Rod Stewart" because of her distinctively raspy vocals. She had major hits in the early '80s with "Total Eclipse of the Heart" and "Holding Out for a Hero." "If You Were a Woman" failed to break the Top 40 chart in the United States when it was released in the spring of 1986. However, it was chart topper in some European countries. It is included on Tyler's album *Secret Dreams and Forbidden Fire*.

Needless to say, "You Give Love a Bad Name" was Bon Jovi's breakthrough smash. It was a song so good that even people that despised hair bands couldn't help but like it. A No. 1 *Billboard* single, it helped propel sales of the album *Slippery When Wet* to well over ten million people.

In retrospect it's not hard to see why one song failed where the other succeeded. Even the most brilliant lyricist would be hard-pressed to come up with coherent lyrics for a song titled "If You Were a Woman (and I was a Man)." On the other hand, "You Give Love a Bad Name" is a great title that lends itself easily to a concise tale of a heartbreaker with looks to kill.

Perhaps "If You Were a Woman (and I was a Man)" would have greater acceptance today, as advances in surgical techniques have made the song's concept entirely feasible!

KISS's "Dreamin'" (1998)

Sounds Like

Alice Cooper's "I'm Eighteen" (1971)

Once upon a time, a young rocker was signed to Frank Zappa's record label. He turned out hard, driving rock and roll albums and later pioneered glam rock while bringing new and exiting theatricality to rock shows. He counted Jim Morrison and John Lennon among his drinking buddies, and Bob Dylan called him one of America's most underrated songwriters. Johnny Rotten sang one of his songs for his Sex Pistols audition and later wrote a glowing essay for an anthology of his material.[18]

Yes, I'm talking about Alice Cooper, a man who's never seemed to get the credit he deserved for his excellent work. A man calling himself Alice was a pretty radical act in 1969. Come to think of it, it would also be a pretty radical act in 2006. Cooper's stage act was pretty far out there, featuring simulated beheadings, mutilated dolls, and a boa constrictor or two.

His mid-'70s stint of hanging out with the likes of Groucho Marx, appearing on TV shows like *Hollywood Squares*, and worst of all, playing golf, didn't

---

18. July 1997. "Ten Questions for Alice Cooper." *Mojo Magazine.*

do much to help his rock credibility. Moreover he broke up his excellent Alice Cooper band in 1974, and his music began to drift into MOR territory.

In spite of all that, Cooper's stage shows were a big influence on many performers, including David Bowie, Marilyn Manson, and KISS.

Speaking of KISS, "Dreamin" sure sounds an awful lot like Cooper's "I'm Eighteen."

How alike are they? Following the release of "Dreamin'" on KISS's *Psycho-Circus* album in 1998, it took Cooper's publisher, Seven Palms Music, only one month to file a plagiarism suit against the song's authors, KISS front man Paul Stanley and former guitarist Bruce Kulick. *Psycho-Circus* reunited KISS's original members—guitarist Ace Freely, drummer Peter Criss, Stanley and lead singer Gene Simmons—in the studio for the first time in years.

These songs are so similar that listening to them back-to-back is almost like listening to the same song twice. The recurring guitar riff, the verses, and the chorus are all very much alike.

A lawyer for Seven Palms claimed the songs were "substantially similar" and expressed hope that the case would be settled out of court. He stated, "It's just a question of whether the KISS people will agree that these songs just sound too much alike. (Paul Stanley is) certainly not going to claim that he never heard 'I'm Eighteen.'"

How could he? "I'm Eighteen" was a No. 21 hit for Cooper in 1971 and has enjoyed widespread FM radio airplay in the years since. The lawsuit was settled out of court in August 1999. The amount of the award to Cooper and Seven Palms was reduced from what they had initially asked due to *Psycho-Circus's* less than spectacular sales performance.[19]

By the way, that song Johnny Rotten sang to get into the Sex Pistols? It was "I'm Eighteen."

---

19. Jaan Uhelszki, *"Coop vs. KISS Case put to Rest."* (Rollingstone.com, August 18, 1999).

Lonestar's "Amazed" (1999)

Sounds Like

Bryan Adams's "Please Forgive Me" (1993)

Lonestar's "Amazed" became a ubiquitous presence on America's radio stations in 1999. It was a perfect pop confection from Nashville's production line—wimpy, inoffensive lyrics, polished production, and a familiar melody. Actually, it's a very familiar melody to anyone who had heard Bryan Adams's "Please Forgive Me," a No. 7 hit from 1993.

The verses of "Amazed" are remarkably similar melodically to the verses of "Please Forgive Me." Lyrically, "Amazed" pays a more than passing resemblance to Adams's massive hit, "(Everything I Do) I Do It for You." Last, the title line at the end of the chorus appears to have been inspired by Paul McCartney's song, "Maybe I'm Amazed."

Interestingly Adams co-wrote "You Walked In," a song that appeared on Lonestar's previous album, 1997's *Crazy Nights*. Adams has enjoyed a semi-secret second career as a songwriter, writing for everyone from Celine Dion to Roger Daltrey. "You Walked In" was written with producer R.J. "Mutt" Lange (aka Mr. Shania Twain).

"Please Forgive Me" is on Adams's greatest hits album, *So Far, So Good*.

"Amazed" was written by Marv Green, Aimee Mayo, and Chris Lindsey. Lindsey also co-authored Lonestar's follow-up No. 1country hit, "Smile."

"Amazed" was one of the most popular songs of 1999. In addition to topping the country chart for almost two months, it was also a No. 1 pop hit. The song won the Country Music Association award for both Song of the Year and Record of the Year for 1999. "Amazed" is on Lonestar's *Lonely Grill* album and helped drive its multi-platinum sales.

Perhaps we shouldn't be too hard on Green, Mayo, and Lindsey. Formula songs like "Amazed" are inevitable in the strictly-formatted world of today's country music radio. Take a bit of this song, a bit of that song, mix it up, and you've got a hit!

Phil Collins's "Everyday" (1994)

Sounds Like

The Human League's "Human" (1986)

Phil Collins was the drummer and eventually the lead singer for Genesis, a group known for its progressive art rock. On the solo albums he began releasing in the early '80s, Collins successfully pursued a more mainstream pop sound. Unfortunately, his sound became so familiar that his songs sometimes sounded like other hits (see "Sussudio").

Phil Oakley and the Human League are best remembered for "Don't You Want Me," a No. 1 hit in 1982, and one of the better songs to come out of the Second British Invasion. This early-'80s invasion saw British new wave bands gain popularity Stateside with the aid of MTV. "Human" was the group's second No. 1 hit.

"Everyday" borrows its recurring synthesizer riff directly from "Human's" chorus. Since the monotonous melody of "Everyday" is a variation of the riff, just about the whole song sounds like "Human."

"Human" was the last hit for the Human League. "Everyday" marked the last time Collins hit the top twenty until 1999's "You'll Be in My Heart."

R.E.M.'s "Drive" (1992)

Sounds Like

David Essex's "Rock On" (1974)

R.E.M. has earned a reputation as one of America's most consistently creative bands since coming on the scene in the early '80s. Therefore we might put this comparison in the category of a knowing nod as opposed to a rip-off.

David Essex was known as a glam rocker and actor, and "Rock On" was his only hit, rising to No. 5 on the U.S. charts. "Rock On" boasts a unique and interesting sound, although it is not played very much on the radio today. It was nominated for a 1974 Grammy

In 1989 TV soap opera star Michael Damian had a No. 1 hit with his cover version of "Rock On."

"Drive" borrows not only "Rock On's" melody but the "Hey, kids, rock and roll" line that accompanies it. The melody recurs in slight variations through-out "Drive."

"Drive" appears on R.E.M.'s *Automatic for the People* CD. The group's next album, 1994's *Monster*, features many references—both musical and lyri-cal—to 1970s glam rock.

In 1998 R.E.M. singer Michael Stipe served as co-executive producer of *Velvet Goldmine*, a movie about the early-'70s British glam-rock scene.

ZZ Top's "La Grange" (1973)

Sounds Like

John Lee Hooker's "Boogie Chillen" (1948)

The similarities between ZZ Top's "La Grange" and John Lee Hooker's "Boogie Chillen" provide a strange case both musically and legally. Hooker's "Boogie Chillen" is a one-chord vamp over which Hooker narrates a tale of arriving in Detroit for the first time. By the time La Cienega Music and Bernard Busman, Hooker's publisher, former producer, and co-writer of "Boogie Chillen," brought a copyright infringement suit in 1992, "La Grange" was almost twenty years old and long a staple of FM radio's classic-rock format.

In comparing the songs, it's important to keep in mind that Hooker had recorded three different studio versions of "Boogie Chillen." The first was recorded for Modern Records in 1948 and became a No. 1 hit on the R & B charts, selling upwards of one million copies. The fact that he received almost no compensation for the sale of these records remained the source of some understandable bitterness for the rest of his life. This less-than-nurturing environment for blues artists led Hooker to record under various pseudonyms in the coming years, including John Lee Booker, Johnny Williams, and Texas Slim. Hooker recorded "Boogie Chillen" again for Vee-Jay Records in 1959 and again with Canned Heat for the *Hooker 'n Heat* album released in 1971. It is the 1971 version that has the most elements in common with "La Grange," including the guitar pattern and the "howl, howl, howl" vocal line.

"La Grange" was on ZZ Top's *Tres Hombres* album and was likely the band's first song to achieve widespread airplay. Besides being a highlight of their concerts, it was included on the *Best of ZZ Top* in 1976 and *ZZ Top's Greatest Hits* in 1992.

ZZ Top's lawyers came up with a clever strategy for fighting the lawsuit. They claimed that "Boogie Chillen" was public domain since its effective copyright date was 1948, when the first recording of the song was released without prior copyright registration. Under the existing law, copyrights were only good for twenty-eight years. Therefore the song's copyright protection had elapsed. The Ninth Circuit Court basically upheld most of these ideas when it ruled that the ZZ Top/La Cienega case would be decided on the basis of the only valid copyright on "Boogie Chillen," the one registered for the 1971 *Hooker 'n Heat* version.[20]

The La Cinega case was settled out of court by ZZ Top in 1997. The Ninth Circuit decision created a loophole that was filled by Congress in 1998 when it revised the 1909 copyright law to clearly indicate that recording a song did not constitute publication for the purposes of the copyright law. This protected the copyright of many songs recorded before 1978 that would have otherwise fallen into public domain.

In his acclaimed biography *Boogie Man*,[21] author Charles Shaar Murray summed up Hooker this way, "John Lee do not do, he be." Yes, Hooker was the real deal—a man whose music grew from the poverty and hardships he had suffered as a young black man in Mississippi. He lived long enough to see a major career revival in the last decade or so of his life. His 1989 album *The Healer* featured guest artists like Bonnie Raitt, Carlos Santana and George Thorogood, and helped introduce him to a younger audience. *The Healer* won the Grammy for Best Contemporary blues album. Soon Hooker was appearing onstage with the Rolling Stones, and was touring with Robert Cray and Los Lobos. Stones guitarist Keith Richards was among the artists appearing on Hooker's 1991 album, *Mr. Lucky*. In 1997 Hooker recorded the album *Don't Look Back* with longtime admirer Van Morrison.

20. LeLand Rucker, "Boogie Fghts," *BluesAccess.com.*, July 1998 edition.
21. Charles Shaar Murray, *Boogie Man: The Adventures of John Lee Hooker in the American Twentieth Century.* (New York: St. Martin's, 2000). 89–90.

Hooker wore one pin of a dollar symbol, because that was what he played for; he wore another in the shape of a star, because he was one. Younger associates were stunned to see the beautiful blonde young women who were always hanging around the octogenarian bluesman.

He died in June 2001 at the age of eighty-three.

The Escape Club's "Wild, Wild, West" (1988)

Sounds Like

Elvis Costello's "Pump It Up" (1978)

Poor Elvis Costello. Although critically acclaimed as one of the most gifted songwriters of his generation, he has never had a top-ten U.S. hit. "Veronica," a song he co-authored with Paul McCartney, came closest, peaking at No. 19 in 1989. Yet he suffered the indignity of seeing the Escape Club's rip-off of one of his most popular songs climb all the way to No. 1.

Costello was a man ahead of his time—by exactly ten years it would appear. Costello's earliest and best albums were widely ignored by radio at the time they were released. Those of you who are old enough can recall what a strange and different sort of figure Costello appeared to be when his first album came out in 1977. With his skinny ties and horn-rimmed glasses, he was an anti-rock star in an era of disco and classic rock.

"Wild, Wild, West" blatantly borrows the music of "Pump It Up's" verses for its own verses. Given the extensive airplay that "Pump It Up" has received in the years since its release, it's hard to think of "Wild, Wild, West" as anything more than a rip-off.

Costello continues to record, but his output has become more introspective and less commercially successful. In 2003 he was deservedly inducted into the Rock and Roll Hall of Fame along with his original backing band, the Attractions.

...AND FURTHERMORE...Costello's music appears to have been influenced by some surprising sources. For instance his classic "Oliver's Army" bears similarities with not one, but two Abba songs. "Dance (While the Music Still Goes On)" is similar in its melody and in the verses. In "Dancing Queen" the similarity lies in the piano flourish introducing the verses.

II

"Not a Second Time?"
Beatles Section

Introduction

The Beatles are the most influential and most imitated rock group ever. In the albums they recorded between 1962 and 1970, you can find a broad range of musical styles, including rockabilly, English dance hall, country, gospel, folk, blues, and even comedy. Most prominent among their legion of disciples in the 1970s were ELO, 10cc, and the decade's most successful performer, Elton John. Power pop bands like Cheap Trick and the Raspberries had a sound and instrumentation based on the Beatles. New wave bands of the late-'70s and early-'80s, such as the Jam, were inspired by the Beatles. In the '90s, the biggest band in the UK was Oasis, a group that worshipped the Beatles to the point of outright imitation.

Beatles references turn up often in modern pop, sometimes in unexpected places. For instance Modern English's "I'll Stop the World and Melt With You" makes direct allusion to the Beatles's "Getting Better" while the Car's "My Best Friend's Girl" borrows its guitar figure from the Beatles's "I Will."

The great success of the Beatles made them a tempting target for those seeking to prove that their songs' copyrights had been infringed. Two such suits were successful. One was against George Harrison for incorporating elements of "He's So Fine" into "My Sweet Lord." The other suit claimed that the Beatles's "Come Together" had ripped off Chuck Berry's "You Can't Catch Me." The Beatles were interviewed about every aspect of their lives. Both John Lennon and Paul McCartney gave extensive *Playboy* interviews in which they broke down the writing of every Beatles song. Lennon later admitted that he may have brought about the "Come Together" suit by citing the Berry influence in an interview.

Who influenced the Beatles? Just about everybody, from English skiffle acts like Lonnie Donnegan, (John was still singing "Rock Island Line" in his apartment at the Dakota in the late '70s) to the original rock and roll acts like

Little Richard, (from whom they adopted the high-pitched "Whooo!" prominent in early songs such as "She Loves You") to the vastly underrated Everly Brothers, who inspired the Beatle's close harmonizing. *The Beatles at the BBC* provides an excellent guide to the band's early influences and includes their covers of a very diverse batch of songs popularized by everyone from Elvis Presley to Anita Bryant.

If you're looking for a very direct influence on the Beatles's music, I would suggest you search out Bobby Parker's "Watch Your Step," a very obscure song from 1961. Both Lennon and Harrison cited this song as the basis for "I Feel Fine." Parker's song probably helped influence the creation of "Day Tripper" as well. "Watch Your Step" so impressed Lennon that he wanted to make a whole album's worth of songs built around Parker's riff. A slight variation of this riff was later used by the Allman Brothers on "One Way Out."

As we shall see, The Beatles soaked up the influences around them, both before and after their rise to fame. Their influence on others was such that almost no one in the music-making business was unaffected by their success. That they remained the biggest band in the world throughout the turbulent 1960s is testament to their openness to change, their continuing desire to innovate, and their immense talent.

The Beatles's "Come Together" (1969)

Sounds Like

Chuck Berry's "You Can't Catch Me" (1956)

In 1973 Chuck Berry's publisher, Big Seven Music, brought a lawsuit against John Lennon claiming that he had plagiarized the music and some of the lyrics of "You Can't Catch Me." The lyrics in question were the opening lines of "Come Together," which mention a "flat top," and are indeed copied from the Berry song almost word for word. The trouble for Lennon was that the melodies of the two songs were also similar.

Berry was a musical godfather to almost all the '60s rock vanguard, including the Beatles (six Berry tunes are among their early BBC recordings), the Rolling Stones (whose early albums consist of numerous Berry covers), and Bob Dylan ("Subterranean Homesick Blues"). "Come Together" certainly has its own distinct sound and feel, and in this sense it really doesn't sound like the Berry recording. Perhaps we may think of it as Berry's straightforward '50s rock filtered through a late-'60s drug haze and Lennon's pop genius

The lawsuit was settled out of court. Lennon, while denying copyright infringement, agreed to record three songs published by Big Seven Music.

One of these tunes was "Ya Ya," the old Lee Dorsey hit that is on Lennon's 1974 *Walls and Bridges* album. The other two were Berry songs and appeared on Lennon's *Rock 'n Roll* album in 1975. They were "Sweet Little Sixteen," and appropriately or ironically, "You Can't Catch Me"

In his 1980 *Playboy*[22] interview Lennon stated his belief that the suit was brought about by the "flat top" line and the fact that he had once admitted[23] that "You Can't Catch Me" had influenced the writing of "Come Together." He went on to claim of "Come Together" that "It's *nothing* like the Chuck Berry song...(it) remains independent of Chuck Berry or anyone else on earth."

It's worth noting that in his highly-praised analysis of the Beatles's work, *Revolution in the Head*, author Ian McDonald posited that "Come Together" was a key statement in understanding the profound cultural changes that the Beatles both instigated and reflected.

22.   David Sheff and Barry G. Golson. *The Playboy Interviews With John Lennon and Yoko Ono*. (New York: Playboy Press, 1981).

23.   Lennon told *Rolling Stone* in 1970: "I was writing like this, 'You Can't Catch Me', the same rhythm and I'm using the old words. I often do it...just make up–parodize the words." Jann S. Wenner, *Lennon Remembers*, (New York: Verso, 2000).

George Harrison's "My Sweet Lord" (1970)

Sounds Like

The Chiffons's "He's So Fine" (1963)

This is easily the most prominent case of copyright infringement in pop music. The case's popularity is due to the fact that both of these songs were No. 1 hits, and the lawsuit was much publicized.

Of course, the songs do sound strikingly similar, even if their separate vibes are worlds apart. To a listener in the year 2006, it is startling to realize that these songs were separated by only seven years time. They can now be seen as bookends to the 1960s, and are evidence of the musical climate shift led by Harrison's former band.

In 1976 a U.S. District Court judge ruled that Harrison had subconsciously plagiarized "He's So Fine" and ruled in favor of the song's copyright holder, Bright Music. The judge's ruling stated, "It is clear that 'My Sweet Lord' is the very same song as 'He's So Fine.'" The judge found not only the familiar first choruses to be the same, but also found similarities in the ensuing verses. Harrison admitted to having heard "He's So Fine," which was a No. 1 hit in the United States and a top-ten hit in the U.K. The case dragged on in the courts for many years, with Harrison eventually purchasing the publishing rights to "He's So Fine." In a 1996 interview,[24] Harrison characterized the entire exercise as a "total joke," and placed the blame at the doorstep of his former-manager Allen Klein.

Trial testimony revealed that "My Sweet Lord" grew out of a jam session that Harrison and Billy Preston held during husband and wife duo Delaney and Bonnie's U.K. tour in December 1969. The trial judge speculated openly that Preston may have had a larger role in the writing of "My Sweet Lord" than he was credited for. Indeed, Preston was the first to record the song in early 1970, with Harrison on hand in the studio. Preston's record was released on the Beatle's Apple label, but failed to chart. This fact would later make it possible for George's lawyers to credibly claim that it was Harrison's talent and notoriety as an ex-Beatle that made "My Sweet Lord" a hit, *not* the melody under copyright to Bright Music.

In an interview with *New Musical Express* in 1977, Harrison reflected on how "My Sweet Lord" was created: "In 1968 the big song was 'Oh Happy Day.' I thought it was great to be able to do something both spiritual and commercial...I wanted to come up with something like that. Incidentally the chord changes on 'My Sweet Lord' and 'Oh Happy Day' are the same...I guess I finally realized that the songs ("My Sweet Lord" and "He's So Fine") sounded similar when (my) song came out on the radio in 1970 and a few disc jockeys got off on the idea...I don't consider it a lift because in my mind I was trying to do 'Oh Happy Day.'"[25]

Harrison's 1976 song, "This Song" takes a tongue-in-cheek look at this case, including the line, "This song has nothing 'Bright' about it." His No. 1 comeback hit from 1988, "Got My Mind Set On You," was a much-revamped cover of an obscure James Ray song from the early 1960s.

Sadly the author of "He's So Fine" was not around to collect his windfall. Ronnie Mack died of Hodgkin's disease shortly after his song became a smash.

Perhaps Harrison summed it up best: "I still don't understand how the courts aren't filled with similar cases—as 99 percent of popular music...is reminiscent of something or other."[26]

---

24.   Bill Ramsey, "So Long, Quiet One," *Seattle Weekly*, December 5, 2001
25.   Lisa Robinson, 12/11/76. "This Song" *New Musical Express*. Reprinted in *Uncut Originals*, 2005.
26.   George Harrison,. *I Me Mine*. (San Francisco: Chronicle Books, 2002.)

Bob Dylan's "Fourth Time Around" (1966)

Sounds Like

The Beatles's "Norwegian Wood" (1965)

This is a bit of a tangled case. Students of Beatle lore are familiar with the fact that John Lennon freaked out the first time he heard Bob Dylan's "Fourth Time Around." To his ears, it sounded like a parody of the Beatles's "Norwegian Wood," which was released only months earlier.[27] The songs are similar in feel and in the story behind the lyrics, though they differ melodically.

A bit of history is necessary to understand the intertwined relationship between the Beatles and Dylan during this time. In the *Beatles Anthology*[28] Paul McCartney said that Dylan became an idol to the Beatles after they heard the *Freewheelin' Bob Dylan* album. Dylan was impressed when he first heard "I Want to Hold Your Hand" on the radio in January 1964. Legend has

---

27. Paul Ed Trynka, *Ten Years that Shook the World*. (New York, London: DK, 2004).
28. The Beatles. *The Beatles Anthology*. (San Francisco: Chronicle Books, 2000).

it that Dylan turned the Beatles on to pot for the first time during a meeting later that year in a New York hotel room. Whatever the case, by early 1965, Lennon was sporting a cap similar to Dylan's and was writing folk-like songs like "You've Got to Hide Your Love Away." In January 1965 he told *Melody Maker* that Dylan had influenced his songwriting: "Anyone who is the best in his field—as Dylan is—is bound to influence people...I wouldn't be surprised if we influenced him in some way."[29]

John went on to claim that "A Hard Day's Night" had started out in a Dylan-like vein. "But it was Beatle-ified before we recorded it."[30]

The summer of '65 saw Dylan go electric at the Newport Folk Festival, and record "Like a Rolling Stone." Both events seemed to be influenced by the music of the Beatles and the Byrds, who took an electrified version of Dylan's "Mr. Tambourine Man" to No. 1 earlier in the year.

In the fall, The Beatles entered Abbey Road studios to record *Rubber Soul*, a groundbreaking album of original songs in which Dylan's influence was heard both musically and lyrically. "Norwegian Wood" was a case in point.

At the same time, Dylan was in a New York City studio recording the song, "I Wanna Be Your Lover," a failed attempt at a single that bore a strong lyrical resemblance to the Beatles's's song, "I Want To Be Your Man." "I Wanna Be Your Lover" didn't see the light of day until Dylan's *Biograph* box set was released in 1985.

Lennon's paranoia upon hearing "Fourth Time Around" probably stemmed from insecurity about making Dylan's influence so obvious in "Norwegian Wood." The title of Dylan's song supposedly refers to the fact that Lennon had recorded three songs wherein the Dylan influence is apparent. "I'm a Loser," "You've Got to Hide Your Love Away," and "Norwegian Wood."

Then there is the intriguing story told by Dylan session player Al Kooper. Asked by Kooper during the recording of "Fourth Time Around" about the tune's obvious similarities to "Norwegian Wood," Dylan claimed that Lennon had based "Norwegian Wood" on "Fourth Time Around," *not* the other way around. Referring to Dylan and the Beatles, Kooper went on: "Evidently he'd played it ('Fourth Time Around') for them, and they'd nicked it! I asked if he

---

29.   Robert Santelli, *The Bob Dylan Scrapbook 1956–1966*. (New York: Simon & Schuster, 2005).

30.   Ibid.

was worried about getting sued by the Beatles and he just said 'They couldn't sue me!'"[31]

"Norwegian Wood" was released on the Beatles's *Rubber Soul* album in early December 1965. Dylan didn't record "Fourth Time Around" until February 1966. Dylan and Lennon shared what appears to be a drug-fueled London cab ride in May 1966, just a week after "Fourth Time Around" was released on Dylan's landmark *Blonde on Blonde* album. This cab ride is documented in D.A. Pennebacker's rarely-seen account of Dylan's 1966 British tour, *Eat the Document*.

The artistic cross-pollination between Dylan and Lennon continued for years. One of Lennon's best songs, 1970's "Working Class Hero," clearly bears the stamp of someone who has spent a lot of time listening to Dylan's early albums. In 1979 Lennon wrote and recorded the song "Serve Yourself" in reaction to Dylan's becoming a born-again Christian. The Lennon *Anthology* box set includes several Dylan parodies wherein Lennon imitates Dylan's singing style. In the liner notes for *Biograph*, Dylan wrote of how much he misses John. Don't we all?

---

31. Andy Gill, "When I Paint My Masterpiece." *Q Dylan Collectors Edition*, (October 2000).

John Lennon & Yoko Ono's "Happy Xmas (War is Over)" (1971)

Sounds Like

George Harrison's "Try Some, Buy Some" (1973)

In his last interview, given two days before his death, John Lennon explained the connection between these songs to BBC interviewer Andy Peebles. The dirge-like "Try Some, Buy Some" was first recorded by Ronnie Spector for her Apple Records debut in 1971. Harrison produced the sessions along with Spector's brilliant but eccentric husband, Phil. When Lennon was recording "Happy Xmas" later that year, he asked Spector to give his song a string backing similar to the one he had provided for "Try Some, Buy Some." Lennon advised listeners to "comparison shop" listening to both songs, saying, "You'll hear the idea for the backing there, which is what we did."[32] Indeed it sounds as though Phil may have used the same charts for both songs. The string sec-

---

32. Lennon and Ono with Andy Peebles. *The Last Lennon Tapes.* (New York: Dell Publishing, 1981).

tions play a prominent role on both records. It can also be noted that Lennon's "#9 Dream" uses the string arrangement from the Lennon-produced Harry Nilson version of "Many Rivers to Cross."

Harrison issued his own version of "Try Some, Buy Some" two years later on his 1973 album, *Living in the Material World*. A word of advice, listen at your own risk.

Spector's single was released in April 1971 and disappeared without a trace. Why? Let's just say that "Try Some, Buy Some" was not "Something." How bad a song is it? It's so bad that when Harrison sang the tune for Spector in the studio she thought he and Phil were playing a joke on her. She thought they were only pretending that she was to record such a lousy song. As she recounts in her autobiography, *Be My Baby*,[33] Spector was mystified by Harrison's obtuse lyrics and thought the finished record "stunk."

Harrison's song, "You," shares a similar history with "Try Some, Buy Some." A backing track for "You" was recorded with Phil Spector in 1971, apparently for Ronnie to use on a potential future album. George later put his own vocals on this track and had a top-twenty hit with "You" in 1975. "You" is an up-tempo song far better suited to Ronnie's style, so it's too bad she didn't get to record it. Then again, it's hard to think of any singer whose style would be suited to "Try Some, Buy Some."

Ronnie has recorded sporadically in the ensuing years, most notably with Eddie Money on the top-five 1986 hit, "Take Me Home Tonight." She recorded a version of Billy Joel's "Say Goodbye to Hollywood" with Bruce Springsteen's E Street Band in 1976. The version deserved to be a smash, but wasn't.

"Happy Xmas (War is Over)" has become a holiday classic and is accorded extensive radio airplay every Christmas season. The song has a melody not dissimilar to that of the folk standard "Stewball," a song recorded by Peter, Paul, and Mary and the Weavers amongst many others.

Phil Spector's reputedly strange lifestyle became the subject of much media attention in early 2003. He was charged in the shooting death of a woman in his Los Angeles-area mansion.

---

33.   Ronnie Spector and Vince Waldron. *Be My Baby*. (New York: Crown Publishing, 1990).

Yoko Ono's "I'm Your Angel" (1980)

Sounds Like

Eddie Cantor's "Makin' Whoopee" (1928)

Yoko Ono's "I'm Your Angel" can accurately be described as a rip-off. Why? Listen to the song. It's a note-for-note copy of Eddie Cantor's "Makin' Whoopee." As reported in Albert Goldman's book, *The Lives of John Lennon,* [34] producer Jack Douglas warned Ono against recording the song in 4/4, as opposed to 3/4 time, saying "you'd be in trouble." Thus we have a case in which the artist had been alerted in advance to a song's similarity to an earlier song. Needless to say, Ono proceeded to record the song in 4/4, claiming she had never heard "Makin' Whoopee."

"Makin' Whoopie" has been recorded by many prominent artists, including Frank Sinatra, Ella Fitzgerald, Louis Armstrong, and Dr. John.

In 1984 the copyright holders of "Makin' Whoopee" brought a multi-million dollar lawsuit against Ono. It was eventually settled out of court.

---

34. Albert Goldman, *The Lives of John Lennon.* (Chicago: A Cappella, 2001).

"I'm Your Angel" was on John and Yoko's *Double Fantasy* album, which was released only weeks before John's December 8, 1980, murder. Another *Double Fantasy* song, Lennon's "(Just Like) Starting Over," shared musical similarities with the Beach Boys's "Don't Worry Baby" and the Guess Who's "Laughing."

The Jam's "Start!" (1980)

Sounds Like

The Beatles's "Taxman" (1966)

Along with the Sex Pistols and the Clash, the Jam was a seminal British punk band. They debuted with the gloriously noisy album, *In the City*, in 1977. Their music was heavily influenced by British bands of the '60s such as the Who, The Small Faces, and the Kinks. Perhaps because of this English sensibility, the Jam never achieved near the level of popularity in the United States that they did in their homeland.

The similarities between "Start!" and "Taxman" are strikingly obvious and were noted in the press at the time. "Start!" borrows the bass, drum, and guitar patterns from "Taxman" and uses this foundation to construct a new song. "Start!" is quite a good track, and something of a departure from the Jam's earlier sound.

"Taxman" is the leadoff track on the Beatles's *Revolver*, often cited among the greatest albums in rock history. "Taxman" is one of three songs on the album that are written and sung by George Harrison. This marked something of a breakthrough for Harrison because he had never had more than two songs on any previous group album. "Taxman" features biting lyrics decrying the British tax system, and an inventive guitar solo played by Paul McCartney.

The Jam's leader and songwriter Paul Weller freely admitted that "Start!'s" guitar pattern had been nicked from "Taxman," but he accurately pointed out that "Start!" has an original melody.

"Start!" went to No. 1 on the British charts and is contained on the Jam's excellent *Sound Affects* album.

Weller broke up the Jam in 1982. He went on to form the jazz/soul duo Style Council with pianist Mick Talbot. The '90s saw Weller return to his rock roots with a series of solo albums including *Stanley Road,* which went to the top of the British charts in 1995. Also in 1995, Weller teamed up with McCartney and Noel Gallagher of Oasis to record the Beatles's "Come Together" for the War Child charity.

The Beatles's "If I Needed Someone" (1965)

Sounds Like

The Byrds's "The Bells of Rhymney" (1965)

The Beatles's "If I Needed Someone," and the Byrds's "The Bells of Rhymney," illustrate the fertile cross-pollination that existed among the Dylan-Byrds-Beatles axis during the mid 1960s. We've already looked at the Beatles-Dylan relationship; here we'll examine the indispensable role of the Byrds in the mix.

Gene Clark quit the New Christy Minstrels after hearing the Beatles's "She Loves You" in 1963. He heard the song while touring Canada in 1963. This meant he was fortunate to be in one of the rare places in North America where the Beatles's single (released on the Swan label when Capitol turned it down) was getting any airplay. He was convinced that the Beatles's sound was the wave of the future, so he headed to Los Angeles to seek out like-minded musicians. There he hooked up with Jim (later known as Roger) McGuinn and David Crosby, both of whom were doing Beatles's songs in their solo acoustic acts.

The classic Byrds's sound was created as a result of the group seeing the Beatles's movie *A Hard Day's Night* in 1964. In the movie, George Harrison's 12-string electric Rickenbacker guitar is featured prominently on several songs, including the title song and "I Should Have Known Better." McGuinn immediately purchased a Rickenbacker 12 string of his own. It was this guitar that, along with gorgeous three-part harmonies, would define the Byrds distinctive sound.

The Byrds recorded Bob Dylan's "Mr. Tambourine Man" in January 1965. Although McGuinn is the only Byrd playing on the track, the song went to No. 1 and effectively gave birth to the folk-rock sound that would dominate the charts in the coming years. It's hard to overestimate the impact of this recording on the music of the 1960s. Dylan's "Blowin' in the Wind" and "Don't Think Twice" were taken into the top ten by Peter, Paul and Mary in 1963, but "Mr. Tambourine Man" marked the first time serious lyrics were wedded to a rock and roll beat.[35] By the summer, Dylan would record "Like a Rolling Stone" and would go electric at the Newport Folk Festival. Perhaps Dylan would have done those things anyway, but the enormous commercial and artistic success of the Byrds recording of his song could only have spurred him on. The Byrds recorded three other Dylan compositions for their debut album *Mr. Tambourine Man*, and the man himself was pictured with the group in a photo on the back cover of the album.

Also recorded for the *Mr. Tambourine Man* album was the Pete Seeger composition "The Bells of Rhymney." Seeger had based the song's lyrics on a poem about a mining accident, yet when the Byrds played the song live at Ciro's in Los Angeles, the dance floor would inevitably fill up. The song featured McGuinn's 12-string Rickenbacker and distinctive harmony singing from Crosby and Clark.

Harrison's composition "If I Needed Someone" is one of those wonderful Beatles's tracks that make you marvel at the level of excellence the Beatles achieved even on songs that were "just" album tracks. One of two Harrison compositions on the Beatles's *Rubber Soul* album, "If I Needed Someone" shows him to be finding his voice as a songwriter who would soon be able to hold his own with Lennon and McCartney. Harrison admitted[36] that "If I

---

35.   Specifically, the beat of the Beach Boys recent hit "Don't Worry Baby," at the suggestion of producer Terry Melcher.

36.   Vic Garbarini, "When We Was Fab." *Guitar World*. January 2001,196– 200.

Needed Someone" had been influenced instrumentally by the "Bells of Rhymney" in its chiming variations around a D chord. It is the guitar pattern that makes the songs sound alike, not the individual melodies. Like "The Bells of Rhymney," "If I Needed Someone" features some fine wordless three-part harmony singing from Lennon, McCartney and Harrison.

Ever the gentleman, Harrison acknowledged his debt to McGuinn directly. He sent a note to the Byrds stating that "'If I Needed Someone' is the riff from 'Bells of Rhymney' and the drumming from 'She Don't Care About Time,'or my impression of it."[37]

McGuinn completed the circle when he recorded "If I Needed Someone" for his 2004 album *Limited Edition*.

One would be remiss not to mention the music of the Searchers and the Animals in discussing the origins of the Byrds's sound. McGuinn has often cited Searchers songs such as "Needles and Pins" and "Every Time You Walk in the Room" (both of which feature a 12-string guitar) as being strong influences as the Byrds's were forming. The Searchers recorded what may be the earliest example of what came to be know as folk rock when they released an electric version of "Where Have All the Flowers Gone" on their debut album way back in the summer of 1963.

The Animals version of "The House of the Sun" was an electrified version of the folk classic that Dylan had recorded for his first album, released in 1962. The Animals cover stayed at No. 1 on the U.S. charts for a month in September 1964. Let's remember that in 1964 The Animals also recorded another electric version of a song from Dylan's first album, "Baby Let Me Follow You Down." It would appear that Dylan was paying attention, since he played a searing electric version of "Baby Let Me Follow You Down" on his legendary 1965–66 tour with the Hawks (aka the Band).

---

37. Johnny Rogan, "Once Upon a Time in the West." *Mojo*, April, 1997, 41.

III

"The Song Remains the Same"
Led Zeppelin Section

Introduction

Despite their massive success and enduring legacy, Led Zeppelin has been the target of plagiarism claims for many years. Since their music was based on American blues, an idiom in which songs were regularly lifted from fellow practitioners, the band could claim that they were merely carrying on in that tradition. The problem was that Zeppelin was operating in a new era wherein songs were protected by copyrights and albums sold in the millions.

Zeppelin routinely claimed credit for songs that they clearly had not written. On their first album, issued in early 1969, they credited "You Shook Me" and "I Can't Quit You Baby" to their author, Willie Dixon. On their second album, issued later that year, they failed to credit Dixon with at least a co-writing credit for either "Whole Lotta Love" or "Bring It on Home," songs that were clearly based on Dixon compositions. Zeppelin's version of "Bring It on Home" is closely based on Sonny Boy Williamson's version. Both of these suits were later settled, and Dixon received compensation and a co-writing credit.

"The Lemon Song" was based on Howlin' Wolf's (aka Chester Burnett) "Killing Floor." In fact, in early concerts, Zeppelin performed "The Lemon Song" under the title "Killing Floor." "The Lemon Song" is different from "Killing Floor" in that Zeppelin guitarist Jimmy Page has supplied a driving riff of his own, and the two songs don't really sound all that alike. Nevertheless a lawsuit was brought by Holwin' Wolf's publisher, and settled out of court.

It is apparent that the first album's "Dazed and Confused" was based on a song called "I'm Confused" by songwriter Jake Holmes. Page performed a revamped version of the Holmes song in 1967 and 1968 with the Yardbirds under its original title. No legal action on behalf of Holmes was ever reported.

Page claimed a copyright on the first album's "Babe, I'm Gonna Leave You," describing it as "Traditional: Arrangement by Jimmy Page." We'll take a further look at that case in this chapter.

Zeppelin seemed to be a bit more generous in crediting its songs as time went on. On the band's fourth album, their mighty version of "When the Levee Breaks" included a one-fifth writing credit to the song's author, Memphis Minnie. In Zeppelin's defense, one might ask if teenage-Zeppelin fans would have ever been exposed to Memphis Minnie's music otherwise.

Physical Graffiti's "Boogie With Stu" was based on Ritchie Valen's "Ooh! My Head."[38] Recorded with Rolling Stones's sideman Ian Stewart, Zeppelin gave a one-fifth writering credit to Mrs. Valens. Unfortunately Valen's mom and the publisher of the song did not think this partial credit was satisfactory, and a lawsuit was brought in 1978. It was later settled out of court for an undisclosed sum.

Page has argued that he always sought to add something new to elements of previous songs that he used with Zeppelin. He's pointed out that Zeppelin singer Robert Plant didn't always change the lyrics from those in the original song, and that caused them a lot of grief. Such was certainly the case with "Whole Lotta Love."

In what can only be thought of as poetic justice, Zeppelin itself has been plundered by many performers. Heart's Ann and Nancy Wilson were devoted Zeppelin fans who appropriated the distinctive guitar riff from "Achilles Last Stand" in fashioning their hit song "Barracuda." In this chapter, we'll examine the more recent case of Pearl Jam borrowing the melody of "Goin' to California" for their song "Given to Fly."

---

38.   Itself a re-write of Little Richard's "Ooh, My Soul."

Led Zeppelin's "Babe, I'm Gonna Leave You" (1969)

Sounds Like

Joan Baez's "Babe, I'm Gonna Leave You" (1962)

The Joan Baez version of "Babe, I'm Gonna Leave You" was written by a very obscure San Francisco folk singer named Anne Bredon. It was included on the popular album, *Joan Baez in Concert Volume 1*.

The credit on the first Zeppelin album carried the credit, "Traditional, Arr. by Jimmy Page." This meant that Page would collect any publishing royalties the song earned.

Unfortunately this "traditional" was copyrighted by Bredon, and it was less than a decade old.

Some confusion may have come from the fact that the *In Concert* album did not mention Bredon's name. Her name is mentioned in the *Joan Baez Songbook*, published in 1964.

These two songs are similar both lyrically and musically. Zeppelin's version develops into a start/stop rave-up toward the end of the song.

Although most reference books state that Page based the Zeppelin piece on the Baez version of the song, it is worth noting that the song was recorded by the Association in 1965 and Quicksilver Messenger Service in 1968.

Bredon bought suit against Zeppelin's publishers in the 1980s. In the years since, reissues of "Babe, I'm Gonna Leave You" the songwriting credit "Page-Plant-Bredon."

In a case of either irony or poetic justice, Chicago later co-opted Zeppelin's "Babe, I'm Gonna Leave You" riff for "25 or 6 to 4."

Led Zeppelin's "Stairway to Heaven" (1971)

Sounds Like

Spirit's "Taurus" (1968)

The continuing popularity of the music Led Zeppelin made some thirty years ago has got to chagrin the band's many critics. As recently as 2001, a piece in the *New York Times*[39] accused Zeppelin of ruining rock music forever during their reign in the 1970s. Perhaps these detractors are missing the fact that there was always more to Zeppelin than the bone-crunching riffs and banshee wails of "Immigrant Song." Many of the band's songs contained quiet acoustic sections amid the electric bombast. Guitarist Jimmy Page drew inspiration from the folk-music revival of the '60s, particularly British guitarists Bert Jansch and Davy Graham. Page sometimes used the alternate tunings favored by these guitarists, notably on the classic "Kashmir."

Nowhere was this acoustic-electric formula more successfully employed than on "Stairway to Heaven," probably the most popular song in the history

---

39.   Howard Hampton, "'70s Rock: The Bad Vibes Continue." *The New York Times.*, ie, "The band's blues-based, folk-tinged heavy metal had a monolithic, unyielding presence that laid out the borders of '70s rock and roll."

of rock music. Page set out to create a sonic tour-de-force for the band and succeeded spectacularly.

Having had "Stairway to Heaven" ingrained into your consciousness for many years, hearing "Taurus" is a bit of shock. The acoustic arpeggio chord pattern played throughout "Taurus" is almost exactly what Page played on "Stairway to Heaven."

The chords in "Taurus" help set a trippy, laid-back vibe and conjure images of a Haight-Ashbury crash pad circa 1967. This spacey instrumental was written by Spirit guitarist Randy California and is contained on Spirit's first album.

Spirit was a Los Angeles band that also included former Rising Sons's drummer Ed Cassidy (California's step-father) and vocalist Jay Ferguson, who had a solo hit in 1978 with the song "Thunder Island."

In his liner notes for the 1996 CD reissue of the first Spirit album, California was quoted as saying that people have repeatedly asked him why "Stairway to Heaven" sounds so much like "Taurus." He went on to mention that Zeppelin had opened shows for Spirit on their first U.S. tour, and Zeppelin had played another Spirit song, "Fresh Garbage," in their set.

Indeed Zeppelin recorded "Fresh-Garbage" for their first album,[40] although to date this recording has not been released. Since "Taurus" and "Fresh-Garbage" are both on the first Spirit album, we can safely say that Page was aware of "Taurus."

California drowned in 1997. Most of the world remains unaware of the secret history behind "Stairway to Heaven."

---

40.   Keith Shadwick, *Led Zeppelin: The Story of a Band and Their Music, 1968–1980*. (San Francisco: Backbeat Books, 2005).

Led Zeppelin's "Whole Lotta Love" (1969)

Sounds Like

Willie Dixon's "You Need Love" (1962)

Dixon's song was recorded by fellow Chicago bluesman Muddy Waters in 1962. Dixon was arguably the finest blues songwriter America has produced. His songs were recorded by the Doors ("Back Door Man") and the Rolling Stones ("Little Red Rooster").

Listening to Waters's recording today will immediately remind a listener of Zeppelin's classic-rock standard. "Whole Lotta Love" was on their 1969 album imaginatively titled *Led Zeppelin II*, and rose to No. 4 on Billboard's singles chart. Between these two recordings came the Small Faces's "You Need Lovin'," recorded in 1965 and credited to band members Steve Marriot and Ronnie Lane. "You Need Lovin'" carries lyrics and music strikingly similar to both Dixon's and Zeppelin's songs.

Dixon apparently never heard "Whole Lotta Love" until the 1980s. When he did, he sued Zeppelin, their publishing company, and Atlantic records, claiming copyright infringement. An impartial musicologist found that "the tone and spirit of 'You Need Love' have been imitated directly in 'Whole Lotta Love.'"

In 1987 the suit was settled out of court[41] with neither side divulging the settlement amount. Zeppelin's *Early Days* compilation, issued in 1997, credits "Whole Lotta Love" to Page-Plant-Jones-Bonham-Dixon.

Page discussed "Whole Lotta Love" with *Guitar World* magazine in 1997: "We got into some trouble because people felt we lifted it from Willie Dixon, but if you took the lyric out and listened to the track instrumentally, it is clearly something new and different—a completely original piece of music."[42]

Dixon helped found the Blues Heaven Foundation which helped older blues artists recover old royalties owed to them. He died in 1992 at the age of seventy-six. Is there any justice in this world? Well, maybe a little…

---

41.   Phil Sutcliffe, "What Goes On," *Mojo*, March 1999, 19.
42.   Brad Tolinski, "Led Zeppelin: Airwaves to Heaven," *Guitar World*, March 1997.

Pearl Jam's "Given to Fly" (1998)

Sounds Like

Led Zeppelin's "Goin' to California" (1971)

This had to be a major source of embarrassment for the guys in Pearl Jam. "Given to Fly" was not some obscure album track but rather the preview single from their highly hyped album, *Yield*. The similarities between "Given to Fly" and Zeppelins "Goin' to California" are obvious and were widely commented on at the time. Musically the verses are nearly identical, with Pearl Jam adding a guitar figure over what sounds like a mumbled "Goin' to California." Due to the prominence of the two bands, this became one of the more publicized sound-alike cases in recent years.

Perhaps Pearl Jam was under pressure from its label to come up with some more radio-friendly material. Since the 1992 release of its debut, *Ten*, each of the band's successive albums leading up to Yield sold less than the one preceding it. *Ten* was not only a critical and commercial success, but also the definitive grunge-rock album. Songs from the album such as "Jeremy" and "Alive" remain radio staples sixteen years after their release on *Ten*.

Pearl Jam had a No. 1 single in 1999 with its cover of, of all things, J. Frank Wilson and the Cavaliers's teen-death weepie, "Last Kiss." This might have been the last song one ever expected to hear out of Pearl Jam, but it caught on with the public and raised money for Kosovar refugees.

In recent years, Pearl Jam has made live recordings of their concerts available for purchase on the Internet or in no-frills CD packages.

Led Zeppelin's "Trampled Underfoot" (1975)

Sounds Like

The Doobie Brothers's "Long Train Runnin'" (1973)

You may think the Doobie Brothers song "Long Train Runnin'" is titled "Without Love," which sounds like it should have been the title to the song. Composed by singer-guitarist Tom Johnston, "Long Train Runnin'" was a No. 8 hit in the United States in the spring of 1973. Even today it has an ubiquitous presence on oldies and classic-rock radio stations.

"Trampled Underfoot" is a great Zeppelin track, but it betrays obvious melodic, rhythmic, and even lyrical similarities to "Long Train Runnin'." "Trampled Underfoot" was released as a single, and was one of the most prominent tracks on *Physical Graffiti*, considered by many fans to be Zeppelin's greatest album.

Purely circumstantial evidence would indicate that "Long Train Runnin'" may have subconsciously influenced the creation of "Trampled Underfoot." Zeppelin was in the United States on tour while "Long Train Runnin'" was on the charts, and it would stand to reason that Zeppelin was aware of the song.

"Trampled Underfoot," along with the other *Physical Graffiti* songs, was recorded between November 1973 and May 1974.

"Trampled Underfoot" was a fan favorite at Zeppelin concerts from its time of release, and has remained so at Robert Plant's solo shows until this day.

IV

"Sticky Fingers"
Rolling Stones Section

The Rolling Stones's "Anybody Seen My Baby?" (1997)

Sounds Like

k.d. Lang's "Constant Craving" (1992)

In the summer of 1997,[43] the Rolling Stones's guitarist Keith Richards was previewing the group's soon-to-be-released album for his daughter and her friends. As the chorus of "Anybody Seen My Baby?" came around, the girls sang, "Con-stant Craaa-ving." Yes, these girls were onto something, for the choruses were unmistakably identical.

You really have to marvel at how out of touch the Stones's Mick Jagger and Richards were at this point in their careers that neither had apparently (so they claimed) heard Lang's song—a widely-aired Top 40 hit five years earlier. What about the Stones's studio production and record company people? I guess it's tough to tell the emperor he has no clothes.

---

43. Mark Scheerer; Correspondent. CNN Report 10/16/97. Included Keith Richards interview wherein he remarked "…If you're a song-writer, it can happen. You know, it's what goes in may well come out."

"Constant Craving" is on Lang's highly successful *Ingenue* album and is her best-known song. She co-wrote "Constant Craving" with Ben Mink. Once the musical similarities in the two songs were pointed out, the Stones camp decided that "Anybody Seen My Baby" composers Jagger and Richards could be exposed to legal action for plagiarizing "Constant Craving."

These days Stones's albums are released accompanied by a carefully prepared corporate marketing strategy. The Stones were preparing for a world tour to promote the album while it was being mastered. Rather than deleting the song from the album, the "suits" agreed with Lang's publishers to give her a one-third writing credit on "Anybody Seen My Baby?" thus making the authorship Jagger-Richards-Lang-Mink. It's safe to say that this will be a one-time collaboration.

Lang said she felt complimented that the Stones's song sounded like her own. Jagger later told *Rolling Stone*, "I really admire k.d. as a singer. I just wasn't familiar with that song."[44]

It says a lot about the diminution of Jagger and Richard's songwriting that "Anybody Seen My Baby?" is by far the best song on the Stones's *Bridges to Babylon* album. Their next album of new material, 2005's *A Bigger Bang*, was an improvement.

---

44. Paul Cantin, *Ottawa Sun*, August 29, 1997.

The Rolling Stones's "The Last Time" (1965)

Sounds Like

The Staple Singers's "This May Be the Last Time" (1961)

The charitable back-to-back listener of the Rolling Stones's "The Last Time" and the Staple Singers's "This May Be the Last Time" will describe the Stones's hit as a reworking of the Staples song. Others might describe it as a rip-off. It's ironic that a song that began life a gospel tune has brought out basic human traits such as thievery and greed. I know what you're thinking…"How shocking…In the *music business*?"

"This May Be the Last Time" had been a part of the Staples's repertoire since the mid-1950s. It is a very slow song with little instrumentation, except for Pops Staples's electric guitar. The similarity with the Stones's song occurs in the chorus, wherein the Stones repeat the exact words found in "This May Be the Last Time," with a very similar melody.

"The Last Time" can be considered a reworking in that the overall feel of the two songs is worlds apart. The Stones's track features the menacing lead guitar of Brian Jones with Keith Richards on rhythm guitar. It is inarguably one of the greatest Stones's tracks ever. "The Last Time" was a turning point in the Stones's career in that it was the first time a Jagger-Richards song had cracked the U.S. top 10. Until this time, Stones's albums featured mostly R & B cover tunes and few originals. A few months later, another of their compositions, "(I Can't Get No) Satisfaction," went to No. 1 and established the Stones as superstars in the United States.

In recent years, Jagger and Richards have admitted that the Staples song was their inspiration for writing "The Last Time." Asked about composing "The Last Time" Richards stated: "I got down on my knees and thanked Pops Staples! As small a hint as it was—because it was basically a rewrite of a gospel song..."[45]

It's worth noting that Richards has sometimes cited James Brown's 1964 recording, "Maybe the Last Time," as the inspiration for the Stones's song. All three songs share the same lyrics in the chorus, but the Stones's and Staples's songs are more similar melodically.

"This May Be the Last Time" was written by Roebuck "Pops" Staples. The Staple Singers were a family gospel group consisting of Pops's children, Pervis, Cleotha, Yvonne, and Mavis. Mavis usually sang lead, and her voice was an important part of the group's success, especially in later years. They started in Chicago in the early '50s and eventually recorded for Vee-Jay records. Their hits from this period include "Uncloudy Day" and "Will the Circle Be Unbroken." "This May Be the Last Time" is included on their 1961 album, *Swing Low*. Asked about the similarities to the Stones's track in 2005, Mavis Staples told *Mojo* magazine: "A girl was interviewing me and she said 'What do you think about the Rolling Stones doing your song?' I said 'What?' She sent me the record and I told Pops. He said 'Now that's beautiful.' We thought it was great. We were flattered. We thought it was great that they were listening to us."[46]

The Staples moved into the secular arena as the 1960s progressed, eventually recording for the Stax label. They had two No. 1 pop hits, 1972's "I'll Take You There" and 1975's "Let's Do It Again." The latter tune was penned by Curtis Mayfield and apparently caused some consternation among long-time gospel fans.

45.　Barney Hoskyns, "Got a Problem? Keith Richards Will Sort You Out Now." *Mojo*. November 1997.

46.　Geoff Brown, "God Bless the Child," *Mojo Magazine*, May 2005, 65.

The Staple Singers were inducted into the Rock and Roll Hall of Fame in 1999. In December 2000, Pops passed away a day short of his eightieth birthday.

In 1997 a British band, the Verve, ran into trouble when they sampled an old orchestrated version of "The Last Time" for use on their song, "Bittersweet Symphony." The obscure version the Verve wanted to sample was put out by the Andrew Loog Oldham Orchestra. Oldham was the Stones's producer/manager until 1967. ABKCO Music boss, the famous/notorious Allen Klein, controls the publishing of most '60s-era Jagger-Richards tunes. He refused the Verve's request for a clearance to use the sample. Since the looped sample was an important part of "Bittersweet Symphony," the Verve were left with no choice but to give ABKCO full-publishing rights to the song. The album on which "Bittersweet Symphony" appeared, *Urban Hymns*, was a major hit around the world, and the song was a hit on both sides of the Atlantic.

So let's wrap up. Group A had a song lifted by Group B. Group C tried to borrow the song from group B, but group B's former manager now controlled the song's publishing. He refused to grant permission for the song to be used, demanded to be paid, and was paid when group C's song became a massive hit. I feel dirty just telling this story. I think I need to listen to some gospel music.

Neil Young's "Borrowed Tune" (1975)

Sounds Like

The Rolling Stones's "Lady Jane" (1966)

Neil Young's "Borrowed Tune" is a unique entry in this book for two reasons: the "borrowing" of an earlier melody is made explicit in the lyrics, and this borrowing is done for the purpose of highlighting the tired state of mind of the new song's narrator.

Neil Young was going through a rough time in late 1973. He was uncomfortable with the massive level of success he had achieved in the previous year with his No. 1 single, "Heart of Gold," and the pop-oriented album, *Harvest*. Like many others, he was disillusioned as the lost promise of the 1960s was now becoming painfully apparent. Shortly before beginning the recording of what became his *Tonight's the Night* album, Young lost two friends, ex-bandmate Danny Whitten and roadie Bruce Berry to drug overdoses. The recordings Young made in the wake of these tragedies were emotionally raw and under produced to the point that Young's record company initially refused to release them.

"Borrowed Tune" exemplifies this dark atmosphere as well as any song on *Tonight's the Night* when Young, accompanied only by his own piano playing, sings his own forlorn lyric to "Lady Jane's" melody.

In December 1973, Young went on tour playing these songs to decidedly mixed reaction. Those expecting to hear "Heart of Gold" were disappointed.

Young went back into the studio in early 1974 to record *On the Beach*, a critical, if not a commercial success. Released in the summer of 1974, *On the Beach* showed that Young was emerging from the doldrums.

When the album finally saw the light of day in 1975, *Tonight's the Night* was praised by critics as one of the best albums of the year. In years since, it has often made lists of all-time greatest albums.

Young must have been a fan of the Stones's album, *Aftermath*, which includes both "Lady Jane" and "Stupid Girl." The latter title was borrowed by Young for a song released on *Zuma*, his follow-up album to *Tonight's the Night*.

V

"They *Can* Take That Away From Me"
Rod Stewart Section

Rod Stewart's "Do Ya Think I'm Sexy" (1979)

Sounds Like

Jorge Ben's "Taj Mahal" (1972)

To those that hear it for the first time, "Taj Mahal" is a revelation. It's immediately obvious that its chorus was appropriated by Rod Stewart for the chorus of "Do Ya Think I'm Sexy."

Jorge Ben has been performing for over forty years. He is probably best known for his composition "Mas Que Nada" which was covered by a wide-range of artists, including Ella Fitzgerald, during the height of samba's popularity in the 1960s. His contemporaries include artists like Gaetano Veloso. Unlike Veloso, Ben's music was not overtly political, and he managed to avoid the persecution Veloso suffered at the hands of Brazil's military dictatorship.

"Taj Mahal" was included on Ben's 1972 album *Ben*. The song was extremely popular in Brazil and other Latin countries. He recorded a live version of the song with Gilberto Gil in 1975. It's likely that Stewart heard the song in one of the London club's where it was a favorite of DJs.

"Do Ya Think I'm Sexy" was on the receiving end of a lot of abuse in 1979. It helped inspire an anti-disco backlash led by Chicago DJ Steve Dahl. Dahl organized an "I Hate Disco Night" at Chicago's Comisky Park during which a large mound of disco records was blown up between games of a doubleheader.

The White Sox forfeited the second game due to the ensuing riot. Dahl even managed a Top forty hit with his parody of the Stewart hit, "Do Ya Think I'm Disco?"

By 1978 disco's popularity was such that artists as diverse the Rolling Stones ("Miss You"), Frank Sinatra ("Night and Day"), the Beach Boys ("Here Comes the Night") and incredibly, the Grateful Dead ("Dancing in the Street") were recording songs with the distinctive four-on-the-floor disco beat. Of course, the Bee Gees were a pop group that had seen their career hit new heights when they started recording dance music in 1975.

"Do Ya Think I'm Sexy" was one of the most successful of all of these cross-over efforts. Written by Stewart and drummer Carmine Appice, it's a very catchy song that details a one-night stand.

The song was a hit all around the world and was No. 1 in the United States for four weeks. The title phrase, though never actually sung during the song, may have helped provoke the backlash against it.

Shortly after the song's release, Ben brought suit against Stewart and Appice, claiming that "Do Ya Think I'm Sexy" had plagiarized "Taj Mahal." Ben won a judgment in the case, and the case was settled with Stewart and Appice agreeing that all future royalties from "Do Ya Think I'm Sexy" would be donated to the United Nation's children's aid organization UNICEF.

Interviewed in 2005, Ben said that although he was glad the profits from "Do Ya Think I'm Sexy" were going to aid the world's children, he was "upset because UNICEF never asked me about the agreement." [47] Regarding Stewart's hit he said: "I have nothing against that song; everyone loved that song. As a musician, though, I am upset because someone stole my work. If he had asked for permission, OK, there would have been no problem."[48]

Ben changed his name to Jorge Ben Jor some years ago. He did so to eliminate confusion that resulted in some of his recording royalties being paid to George Benson.

FUN FACT: In a sign that the end times may indeed be at hand, in 2006 Paris Hilton revealed that she has recorded "Do Ya Think I'm Sexy" for a forthcoming CD.[49]

---

47. Laura Emerick, "That Man From Rio Finally Makes His Way to Chicago," *Chicago Sun-Times*, February 20, 2005.

48. Ibid.

49. Lawrence Van Gelder, "Arts, Briefly." *New York Times*, May 31, 2006.

Rod Stewart's "The Killing of Georgie" (1976)

Sounds Like

The Beatles's "Don't Let Me Down" (1969)

In addition to claiming that the Rolling Stones had copped their hit, "Miss You," from his 1974 song "Bless You,"[50] John Lennon told *Playboy* in 1980 that the coda of "Georgie" was taken from his Beatles's song "Don't Let Me Down." John was right in claiming the passages were identical. He went on to note ruefully how the "lawyers never noticed."[51] As on the Beatles's track, the same phrase is repeated three times before Stewart varies it on the fourth.

Often considered the archetypal rock star and a target of punk rockers in the '70s, Stewart deserves credit for his courage in recording this sad tale of a New York gay bashing by a New Jersey gang. This subject was rarely, if ever, tackled by Stewart's contemporaries, before or since. The song's sympathetic

---

50. See: Sheff & Golson. Readers may judge this claim for themselves.
     John claimed that "Miss You" was basically a sped-up version of his
     song from the *Walls and Bridges* album. The author doesn't quite hear it.
51. Ibid.

portrait of a gay man was way ahead of its time for the rock and roll world of 1975. The fact that it is based on an actual event makes it all the more poignant.

"Georgie" was on Stewart's hugely successful 1976 album, A *Night on the Town*. It was released as a single and rose to No. 30 in the spring of 1977.

The Beatles's "Don't Let Me Down" was released in May 1969 as the B-side of "Get Back," a No. 1 single. It was recorded during the troubled *Let it Be* sessions in early 1969. The 45 is notable in that it was credited to "the Beatles with Billy Preston," making it the first and only time the Beatles shared billing with another artist on one of their records. Preston's fine electric piano work is prominent on both tracks.

In 2003 "Don't Let Me Down" was included on a revamped version of the Beatles *Let it Be* album. The release of the new version of the album was a tacit rebuke of the work Phil Spector had done in assembling the original *Let it Be* album. The inclusion of "Don't Let Me Down" is apparently one of these corrections. While the song fits in easily with the other songs on the album, some were troubled by the notion of someone (even Paul McCartney) tampering with the Beatles's classic albums.

Rod Stewart's "Forever Young" (1988)

Sounds Like

Bob Dylan's "Forever Young" (1973)

Rod Stewart's "Forever Young" and Bob Dylan's "Forever Young" are more alike lyrically than musically. Stewart's song is lyrically structured to be almost identical to Dylan's—from the "May you..." lines of the verses, to the repeated title in the chorus. Stewart provides a different melody line, but his song is obviously based on Dylan's.

Details are sketchy, but the similarity did not escape the ears of Dylan's publisher. Originally credited to Stewart and sidemen Jim Cregan and Kevin Savigar, Stewart's "Forever Young" is credited to Stewart-Cregan-Savigar-Dylan on subsequent releases. The song has been released on several Stewart compilations, including the *Storyteller* box set and a 2001 *Best of.*

Dylan's "Forever Young" is on *Planet Waves*, an album that he recorded with the Band prior to reuniting with them for a successful U.S. tour in 1974. Although never released as a single, "Forever Young" has received extensive airplay over the years, and is one of the better known Dylan recordings of the

1970s. Dylan performed "Forever Young" at the Band's 1976 *Last Waltz* fare-well concert, an event immortalized on film by Martin Scorcese.

Stewart was no stranger to Dylan's work. In fact, an argument could be made that Stewart is of the finer interpreters of Dylan's material. Among the Dylan songs Stewart has recorded are "Only a Hobo," "Mama, You've Been on My Mind," "Just Like a Woman," "Sweetheart Like You," and "Girl of the North Country." Had this case gone to court, Stewart would have been hard-pressed to deny his familiarity with Dylan's "Forever Young," given that he has recorded some of the more obscure items in the Dylan songbook.

KISS's "Hard Luck Woman" (1976)

Sounds Like

Rod Stewart's "You Wear It Well" (1972)

KISS was the most popular American band of the mid-1970s. This was largely due to their energetic live performances, over-the-top theatrics, and good, hard-rocking songs. The fact that all four members wore make-up masks contributed to their music being taken less than seriously by most critics. In retrospect their influence is clearly present in the music of bands as diverse as Van Halen (originally discovered by KISS's Gene Simmons), Metallica, and Nirvana. KISS's hipster credentials got a shot in the arm when the Replacements covered "Black Diamond" on their *Let It Be* album in 1984.

Often caricatured as metal goofs, KISS actually flirted with other genres of music, including disco, ("I Was Made for Loving You"), ballads, ("Beth," a No. 7 hit in 1976 which may hold the dubious distinction of being first power ballad), and folk rock. That brings us to "Hard Luck Woman."

KISS blatantly copied the opening-guitar figure from "You Wear It Well" to introduce "Hard Luck Woman." The band then constructed a new song—a song with a similar rhythm to that of "You Wear It Well"—over that guitar pattern.

"You Wear it Well" is on Stewart's highly successful 1972 album, *Never a Dull Moment*. As a single it reached No. 13 on the Billboard chart, and has been widely played on FM radio ever since.

"Hard Luck Woman" was released on KISS's *Rock and Roll Over* album, and reached No. 15 on the singles chart. In 1996 Garth Brooks, then at the height of his massive popularity, recorded a song with KISS[52] for the band's tribute album, *Kiss My Ass*. The song he chose was a very faithful cover of "Hard Luck Woman."

52.   David Leaf and Ken Sharp, *Kiss: Behind the Mask*. (New York: Warner Books, 2003).

VI

Would You Believe?

Nirvana's "Smells Like Teen Spirit" (1991)

Sounds Like

Boston's "More Than a Feeling" (1976)

In the summer of 1991, while recording songs for its album *Nevermind*, Nirvana's Krist Novaselic and Kurt Cobain were concerned that "Smells Like Teen Spirit" copied the sound of a favorite band of theirs from Massachusetts. The Pixies, a band that included Frank Black and Kim Deal, had built a loyal following in the late '80s with a sound based on loud guitars and good songs. Many of their songs used a quiet-verse/loud-chorus formula to dramatic effect. Cobain used this technique not only on "Smells Like Teen Spirit" but on other *Nevermind* songs like "Lithium" and "In Bloom."

In 1993 Nirvina even brought in Pixies's producer Steve Albini to produce their third album, *In Utero*, the last Nirvana album released while Cobain was still alive.

Nevermind became a phenomenal success upon its October 1991 release and stayed in the No. 1 slot for weeks. "Smells Like Teen Spirit" was by far the most widely-played track from the album and reached No. 6 on the singles chart in January 1992. Several reviewers commented on its similarity to a song that was not by the Pixies. It was by another band from Boston with a slightly less-hip reputation.

Yes, the chords that make up the guitar patterns of Boston's "More Than a Feeling" and Nirvana's "Teen Spirit" are very similar, but not exact. It is this crunching pattern that kicked off "Teen Spirit" and gave most listeners their introduction to Nirvana's music. In a 1991 appearance at the Reading Festival in England, Nirvana played a very brief version of "More Than a Feeling" before launching into "Smells Like Teen Spirit."[53]

In describing how "Teen Spirit" was created, Cobain said "it was such a cliché riff...so close to a Boston riff. When I came up with the guitar part Krist (Novaselic) looked at me and said 'that's so ridiculous!'"[54] Fans didn't find it ridiculous. Nirvana's album *Nevermind* ended up selling over six million copies in the United States alone, and "Teen Spirit" became an anthem for disaffected youth around the world.

Even though "Teen Spirit" and "More Than a Feeling" are in different keys, and Cobain was not as technically proficient a guitarist as Boston's Tom Scholz, the songs' central guitar patterns still bear a strong resemblance. Asked about the similarities in 1994, Scholz told *Guitar World:* "If that song does sound like 'More than a Feeling' I take it as a major complement, even if it was completely accidental."[55]

"More Than a Feeling" has been a ubiquitous presence on FM playlists since its release on Boston's self-titled debut album in 1976. Boston has released only five albums since then, but their debut album was a multi-million seller. In fact *Boston* may be credited (or blamed) for starting the classic-rock format heard on so many stations today.

Nevermind signaled a sea change in American rock. The hair bands of the '80s could no longer get arrested as Seattle grunge-rock bands like Pearl Jam, Soundgarden, and the like dominated the airwaves and MTV. In retrospect, Nirvana's music seems to have little in common with Pearl Jam's, but it was easy media shorthand to group both bands under the grunge banner. At this time the media coincidentally discovered the existence of a Generation X group of twenty-somethings who apparently spent their days wearing flannel, sipping lattes at Starbucks, and grooving to their favorite grunge-rock groups.

---

53.   Charles R. Cross, *Heavier Than Heaven: A Biography of Kurt Cobain.* (New York: Hyperion 2001).
54.   Peter Henderson, "Titanic" *Mojo Magazine*, May 1998.
55.   February 1995. *Guitar World.* 'Peace of Mind."

Nirvana's music and Cobain's surprisingly poetic lyrics resonated deeply with many young people who were identified by the alienation they expressed. This point was brought home to many only after Cobain's suicide in April 1994.[56] Nirvana died with him, but intriguing hints as to what direction the band may have pursued can be found on the *Unplugged in New York* CD. The CD features the band playing acoustic versions of their music with a cellist, plus covers of David Bowie and Leadbelly songs.

To an outsider, it would appear that Cobain was unprepared for the massive success and worldwide fame that *Nevermind* brought him. His suicide ensured his status as a tragic hero who couldn't fake it anymore.

Cobain once described Nirvana's music as "The Knack and the Bay City Rollers being molested by Black Flag and Black Sabbath."[57] In other words, Nirvana played poppy melodies and tight song structures overlaid with punk attitude and screaming guitars. Cobain had no problem with pop music, but one wonders if a diehard Nirvana fan will ever hear "Teen Spirit" quite the same way after realizing its lineage.

---

56. Cobain makes a reference to heroin use in the first line of the third verse of "Smells Like Teen Spirit."
57. See Cross.

John Lennon's "Imagine" (1971)

Sounds Like

Freddie Lennon's "That's My Life" (1965)

Alfred "Freddie" Lennon abandoned his wife, Julia, and son, John, when the future Beatle was just a baby. John's mother later left John with her sister, Mimi, who provided John with a loving home for the rest of his childhood. Julia was hit by a car and killed when John was seventeen. As a result, John went through his early adult years with a chip on his shoulder, feeling that he had been abandoned twice by his mother.

Freddie's fate provides one of the more obscure corners of Beatles history. Following the phenomenal worldwide success of his son's band in 1964, Freddie turned up granting interviews to the press with a sob story about his desire to speak with his long-lost son. At the time, he was working in a hotel outside of London for £10 a week. In late 1965, Freddie cut a record called "That's My Life (My Love and My Home)." This autobiographical number—the title of which seemed to play off of the Beatles's "In My Life"—featured Freddie speaking poignantly about his love for the sea. Freddie didn't have much to offer in the vocal department, though his speaking voice is eerily similar to John's.

Here the story really gets weird. Listening to "That's My Life," a listener is struck by the similarities to John's song, "Imagine," a song generally thought to be one of John's classic pieces and certainly the best song of his post-Beatles years. The two songs share the same stately tone, and the chords in the verses sound exactly the same. According to Kristofer Engelhardt's book, *Beatles Undercover,*[58] John used to amuse friends by playing "That's My Life," so it seems he had some familiarity with his dad's record. It is likely that, as Engelhardt suggests, "Imagine" was inspired on a subconscious level by Freddie's recording.

"Imagine" is a rock classic, a touchingly idealistic anthem that considers metaphysical concepts of how we should live our lives. How strange that the song perhaps most closely associated with John today had its roots in a crass rip-off of a novelty record made to cash in on a relative's fame.

Freddie went on to have something of a rapprochement with John. In the late '60s, the father and son spent more time together and John purchased a cottage in Brighton for Freddie and his very young bride. Freddie fathered a son named David in 1969, giving John a half-brother at the age of twenty-eight. Freddie died in 1976.

---

58. Kristofer Englehardt, *Beatles Undercover.* (Burlington Ontario, 1998).

Bob Marley and the Wailers's "Buffalo Soldier" (1980)

Sounds Like

The Banana Splits's "The Banana Splits Theme," aka "The Tra La La Song" (1968)

No, the author has not ingested the brown acid. Could reggae great Bob Marley Could Reggae great Bob Marley and a mostly forgotten Saturday morning TV show really have something in common? How could songs of such dissimilar origins appear to share so much musically? Could there be any possible relationship between them? Let's investigate.

The Banana Splits Adventure Hour was a kid's show that ran on NBC from 1968–1970.[59] It showcased the adventures of Bingo, Drooper, Snoorky, and Fleegle, four stuffed animals that played in a band. It took some inspiration from the success of the Monkees's TV show, and likewise utilized the talents of successful songwriters, including Gene Pitney, Barry White, and, in the

---

59. Alex McNeil, *Total Television: The Comprehensive Guide to Programming From 1948 to the Present.* (New York: Penguin Books, 1996), 73.

118

case of the "The Tra La La Song," Mark Barkan and Richie Adams. Songs from the show were released on albums by the Banana Splits, and "The Tra La La Song" was actually a single that dented the lower regions of the Billboard Hot 100.

In 1979, a cover version of "The Tra La La Song" by the Dickies, a U.S. punk band, was a hit in Britain.

"Buffalo Soldier" appeared on Marley's *Uprising* album, released a year before his death. The song tells the little known story of the black U.S. soldiers who fought against Native Americans in the years after the Civil War. The irony of two oppressed peoples fighting against each other is not lost on Marley as he constructs a cautionary tale in which he reminds the listener to remember their history. In the middle, and again at the end of "Buffalo Soldier," Marley breaks into a wordless note-for-note rendition of—of all things—the "Banana Splits Theme."

So what, you ask? Marley couldn't possibly have seen the *Banana Splits* while living in Jamaica. That's probably true, but many are not aware that Marley lived with his mother, Cedella, in Wilmington, Delaware, during several periods of the 1960s. One of these was from April–October 1969, when he could have seen the *Banana Splits* on TV or heard the theme song on the radio.[60] This was an interesting period of Marley's life in that his wife and young children accompanied him to Wilmington. Did he watch Saturday morning TV with his kids?

Marley supported his family by working on a Chrysler assembly line. He returned home in October due to twin desires: to resume his musical career in Jamaica, and to avoid being drafted into the U.S. Army at the height of the Vietnam War.

---

60. Timothy White, *Catch a Fire: The Life of Bob Marley*, (New York: Henry Holt & Company). Also
    Boot and Salewicz *Bob Marley: Songs of Freedom*. (New York: Viking 1995).

Would You Believe?

Kraftwerk's "Autobahn" (1974)

Sounds Like

The Beach Boys's "Fun, Fun, Fun" (1964)

A persuasive argument can be made that Dusseldorf, Germany's, Kraftwerk was the most influential band of the 1970s. Their synthesizer-and-drum-machine sound laid the basis for much of the music of the '80s and '90s. The group started life as a progressive rock band, but soon adapted the minimalist style associated with avant-garde composers like Steve Reich.

Kraftwerk's music can now be seen as a direct influence on at least three musical genres, as writer Andy Gill has pointed out:[61]

1. Eighties Pop

The new romantic or second British Invasion bands of the early 1980s use of sequencers in songs such as "Don't You Want Me" by the Human League (1982) or "Cars" by Gary Numan (1980) owe an obvious debt to Kraftwerk's

---

61. Andy Gill, "Kraftwerk," *Mojo Magazine*, April 1997.

work. Later bands such as Erasure, New Order and Depeche Mode took the sound in a more danceable direction. In fact by 1984, almost all rock records made use sequenced-or sampled-drum sound, eg, Prince's "When Doves Cry" and Bruce Springsteen's "Dancing in the Dark"

2. Hip-hop

Afrika Bambaataa's "Planet Rock" was a seminal hip-hop song recorded in 1982. Bambaataa sampled Kraftwerk's "Trans-European Express" and "Numbers" to provide the background music for his own song. This cross-pollination of musical styles resulted in a breakthrough for hip-hop music, the most prominent musical genre of the past twenty years. Kraftwerk's recordings have been sampled many times by hip-hop artists since "Planet Rock."

3. Techno

Techno pioneer Derrick May described his music as "Kraftwerk and George Clinton trapped in an elevator with one sequencer between them."[62] Techno is far more popular in Europe than in the United States, but has now become part of the mainstream with artists like U2 and Madonna incorporating it into their music.

"Autobahn" was the first Kraftwerk song to include vocals and makes direct reference to "Fun, Fun, Fun" in the chorus. The song took up twenty-two minutes on the *Autobahn* album, but was edited down to three minutes for the single release. The words in German are *"fahr'n, fahr'n, fahr'n auf der autobahn"* (drive, drive, drive on the autobahn), but many listeners heard it as "fun, fun, fun on the autobahn." Thus many listeners were reminded of the Beach Boys classic "Fun, Fun, Fun." The Beach Boys connection was widely commented on by DJs playing "Autobahn" and undoubtedly was a factor in getting "Autobahn" to No. 25 on the U.S. Billboard chart. "Autobahn" sounded nothing like other records on the charts at the time, but more like records that made the charts ten or twenty years later. Thus if you listen to it today, it's perhaps the only charted song from the 1970s that doesn't immediately sound dated. "Autobahn" can be described as a sonic car ride with synthesizers simulating the low rumble of the tires on the road and cars whizzing past.

Kraftwerk leader Florian Schneider cited the Beach Boys as a major influence on the band's music, but the similarities between "Autobahn" and "Fun, Fun, Fun" were probably just coincidental.

---

62. Ibid.

VII

Songs They Stole From Themselves

John Fogerty's "The Old Man Down the Road" (1985)

Sounds Like

Creedence Clearwater Revival's "Run Through the Jungle" (1970)

Can you steal something from yourself? Logic tells us you cannot. But logic doesn't always prevail in our judicial system, much less in the wacky world of the music business. John Fogerty wrote both Creedence Clearwater Revival's "Run Through the Jungle" and his own "The Old Man Down the Road." But he signed away his Creedence-era publishing rights to Fantasy Records honcho Saul Zaentz. Thus he ended up being sued for plagiarizing his own song.

Fogerty and company were known as the Golliwogs when they were signed to Fantasy in 1964. Fantasy was based in Berkeley, California, and was known for its stable of prominent jazz artists. Creedence became one of the most successful American bands of the late '60s and early '70s with a string of seventeen Top 40 hits. Fogerty was the band's lead singer, lead guitarist, and chief songwriter, composing such classics as "Proud Mary," "Fortunate Son," "Green River," and "Bad Moon Rising."

"Run Through the Jungle" was the B-side of "Up Around the Bend," and both songs were on Creedence's excellent *Cosmo's Factory* album, released in 1970. The single rose to No. 10 on the charts that summer. Dissension began to plague the band as tension developed between Fogerty and his bandmates, including his guitarist brother Tom. The 1971 hit "Have You Ever Seen the Rain?" was John's plea to the band to stop their infighting. In other words, they were causing rain to fall on a "sunny day."

The band split for good in 1972 following the release of the less-than-great *Mardi Gras* album. Fogerty was free, but Zaentz retained the rights to his songs under terms of the prohibitive earlier contract.

Fogerty had moderate commercial success with two solo records in 1973 and 1975. "The Old Man Down the Road" is on Fogerty's *Centerfield* album. Released in 1985, it marked his return from a ten-year hiatus from recording. Fogerty proved that his roots-rock style had never really gone out of fashion as the album went to No. 1 and the song went to No. 10. Fogerty included a "love note" on the album to his former record company boss in the form of "Zanz Kant Danz." A song on the album called "Mr. Greed" also appeared to have been inspired by Zaentz. The Fantasy Records honcho was less than amused and sued Fogerty for $142 million, claiming to have been defamed by the "love note" and also claiming that "The Old Man Down the Road" was a rip-off of the Zaentz-owed "Run Through the Jungle."

By this time Zaentz was a bona fide Hollywood mogul, having produced such flicks as *One Flew Over the Cuckoo's Nest,* for which he won an Oscar, and *Amadeus.*

The two songs do have some things in common. The guitar licks that propel both are similar, as are portions of the verses. The chorus sections of the songs are not so alike. Fogerty won the 1988 trial due in part to his courtroom performance of both songs on his guitar. He effectively demonstrated the differences in the two tunes.[63]

Fogerty was awarded one million dollars in attorney fees in 1994. As part of the previous settlement, "Zanz Kant Danz" had become "*Vanz* Kant Danz" on the *Centerfield* album. Zaentz was awarded a second Oscar in 1997 when the *English Patient* won Best Picture.

---

63. For trial background see Bordowitz, Hank. *Bad Moon Rising: The Unofficial Biography of Creedence Clearwater Revival.* (New York: Schirmer Books, 1998).

Fogerty followed up *Centerfield* with *Eye of the Zombie* in 1986. He did not release another album until 1997's *Blue Moon Swamp*, an artistic if not a commercial success.

For more than fifteen years following the breakup of Creedence, Fogerty refused to play any of his old Creedence songs during his live appearances. That changed when he played a Vietnam veterans' benefit in 1987. By 1997 he seemed to have come to terms with the fact that the songs he created were loved by the public, and he performed them with his old fire on his critically acclaimed tour.

In 1999 Fogerty was on tour again. Ex-Creedence members Stu Cook and Doug Clifford toured under the name, Creedence Clearwater Revisited, after Fogerty's lawsuit to prevent their using that name proved unsuccessful. The bitterness continued when the band was inducted into the Rock and Roll Hall of Fame, with Fogerty refusing to appear with Clifford and Cook. In 2004 Fogerty released *Déjà Vu All Over Again* and performed on the "Vote For Change" tour along with Bruce Springsteen and others.

Zaentz isn't doing too badly in the new century either. He owns the film rights and merchandizing on the *Lord of the Rings* movies.

Paul McCartney's "Little Bubble" (2001)

Sounds Like

The Beatles's "Piggies" (1968)

Yes, I know "Piggies" is a George Harrison song, but Paul McCartney was in the group, wasn't he? As with the case of the Rolling Stones's "Anybody Seen My Baby," you have to wonder how a major artist can record a song that is so melodically similar to another song without a producer, engineer, or bandmate pointing out the similarity to the writer. This case is particularly baffling considering the Beatles's work is so well known and has been analyzed ad infinitum for more than thirty years. The fact that the artist in this case is an ex-Beatle makes it ever more curious.

Of course this was not the first time McCartney or the other Beatles had made reference to the group's work in their solo recordings, however, it was usually done with lyrical references. For instance McCartney recorded "Tomorrow" in 1971, an obvious nod to the Beatles "Yesterday," as was his 1992 song "Here Today," a tribute to John Lennon that employed a string quartet arrangement similar to the one on "Yesterday." Harrison recorded "Here Comes the Moon," an allusion to his Beatles's composition "Here Comes the Sun." Harrison's 1988 hit "When We Was Fab" made musical and instrumental references to the Beatles's psychedelic-era music.

"Little Bubble" has no such obvious reference point and appears to be influenced by "Piggies" on a subconscious level. The two songs share a very similar melody line in their choruses. Asked about this by reporter Roger Freidman, McCartney said, "We didn't realize it (the similarity between the two songs) until it was recorded. It's just that one area...but it was just in my head, and I didn't realize it."[64]

Driving Rain also includes the song "Riding Into Jaipur" which features sitars and harkens back to Harrison's Indian-influenced Beatles songs like "The Inner Light" and "Within You, Without You."[65]

A month before his death in November 2001, Harrison reportedly held a bittersweet final meeting with McCartney and Ringo Starr at Staten Island Hospital in New York. Harrison had gone there in a desperate search for treatment for his brain cancer.

Meanwhile, McCartney was promoting *Driving Rain*, the album that contains "Little Bubble." He headlined the charity concert at Madison Square Garden in October 2001 to raise money for the families of the police, fire, and rescue workers lost on September 11. His *Driving USA* tour was the highest grossing U.S. concert tour of 2002.

In November of that year, McCartney joined with Eric Clapton, Ringo Starr, Monty Python members, and others at the Harrison tribute concert held in London's Royal Albert Hall. During the show, later released on DVD as the *Concert for George*, McCartney performed the Harrison compositions "For You Blue" and "All Things Must Pass."

Baby boomers saw Harrison's death as a sad reminder of the passage of time and their own mortality. Although he was only fifty-eight, he had been a part of people's lives for nearly forty years. His inventive guitar work and vocals remain an under-appreciated element in explaining the success of the Beatles's recordings.

---

64. Roger Freidman, FoxNews.com, November 26, 2001.
65. Some listeners noted the resemblance of McCartney's 1993 song "Hope of Deliverance" to "New Blue Moon," a song George recorded with the Travelling Wilburys in 1990.

The Knack's "Baby Talks Dirty" (1980)

Sounds Like

The Knack's "My Sharona" (1979)

Few bands ever experience the spectacular success that greeted the Knack upon the release of their first album, *Get the Knack*, in the summer of 1979. Even fewer experience the critical backlash that was visited upon them soon thereafter. The Knack's first single, "My Sharona," was familiar to anyone near a radio that summer. It stayed at No. 1 for six weeks and was Billboard's biggest hit of the year. So what happened?

It's important to remember that Top-40 radio was firmly in the grip of the disco craze in 1979. Meanwhile artists like the Clash, Elvis Costello, and the Talking Heads had a hard time getting their music heard on the radio. With the British Invasion-influenced pop of *Get the Knack*, the Knack succeeded where these more talented bands did not. This caused resentment among rock's taste-making journalists, and soon the Knack were deemed unhip. To paraphrase Morrissey, we hate it when our friends become successful.

Vanilla Ice suffered a similar fate a decade later when he was deemed to be an unworthy representative of rap, an emerging form of music, just as the

Knack were thought to be unworthy of carrying the new wave banner. Someone even started a tongue-in-cheek "Knuke the Knack" campaign.

This is not to suggest that the Knack didn't bring some of this upon themselves. Their music was tuneful, but derivative. The photos on the album seemed to suggest that they thought themselves to be the next Beatles. They took their name from the film that Richard Lester made after directing the Beatles in *A Hard Day's Night*.

Moreover the Knack didn't seem to take much care with their follow-up album,...*But the Little Girls Understand*. Instead of milking *Get the Knack* for a couple more singles, the second album was recorded in a week and released a mere eight months after the first. Worse yet, the first single from the album was a transparent "My Sharona" rewrite, "Baby Talks Dirty." It's as if the Knack figured that to have another hit like "My Sharona," they had to record a song that sounded like "My Sharona." Unfortunately, "Baby Talks Dirty" only rose to No. 38, and the Knack broke up (for a while) in 1981.

It may not be fair to single out the Knack for trying to replicate the sound of a hit single, a tactic that's been used many times by many different performers, but "Baby Talks Dirty" helped precipitate one of sharpest declines in popularity that any band has ever seen.

VIII

The Oasis Game

The Oasis Game

Match the Oasis song with the song that "inspired" it.

1. "The Masterplan"

2. "She's Electric"

3. "Stand By Me"

4. "Shakermaker"

5. "Morning Glory"

6. "Cigarettes & Alcohol"

7. "All Around the World"

8. "The Swamp Song"

A. "Hey Jude"
The Beatles (1968)

B. "I'd Like to Teach the World to Sing"
New Seekers/Hillside Singers (1971)

C. "On the Road Again"
Canned Heat (1968)

D. "Bang a Gong"
T Rex (1971)

E. "Taurus"
Spirit (1967)

F. "While My Guitar Gently Weeps"
The Beatles (1968)

G. "The One I Love"
R.E.M. (1987)

H. "All the Young Dudes"
Mott the Hoople (1972)

Answers

1. E. "The Masterplan" is an instrumental closely related in melody and mood to Spirit's "Taurus." As we've seen, Led Zeppelin borrowed the opening instrumental passages of "Stairway to Heaven" from "Taurus."

2. F. "She's Electric" borrows its bridge from the "While My Guitar Gently Weeps." The verses bear more than a passing resemblance to the Beatles's "With Help from My Friends."

3. H. The chords in the chorus of "Stand By Me" are obliviously referring to Mott the Hoople's classic "All the Young Dudes," a song David Bowie wrote for them.

4. B. The song borrows musically and lyrically from the song that began life as a Coke commercial in 1971. In what is know to this day as one of the most successful ad campaigns of all time, Coke gathered people of various ethnic backgrounds on a mountainside to sing "I'd like to Teach the World to Sing." The subtext of the ad was that world peace could be achieved if only people could enjoy cola together. People liked and requested the song so much that a version was recorded minus the Coke references.

5. G. "Morning Glory" has its own melody, but the main guitar riff is borrowed from R.E.M.'s first hit single, "The One I Love."

6. D. "Bang a Gong" was a No. 1 record in the UK and a top ten hit in the United States. It's from T-Rex's classic album *Electric Warrior*. The song was also a big hit in the 1980s for the Robert Palmer-led band Power Station.

7. A. The long concluding section of "All Around the World" might be called "Hey Jude-esque." Not an exact copy, but clearly drawing inspiration from the Beatles's smash. In 2006 "All Around the World" was widely heard in AT&T's television commercials.

8. C. Lead guitarist and songwriter for Oasis, Noel Gallagher admitted that "Swamp Song" is based on the Canned Heat classic—a fact apparent to anyone with two ears.

IX

New Music?

Maybe it's that rock and roll has been around so long. Maybe it's that this author has been around so long. Either way it sure seems that new rock music is increasingly referential to earlier songs, and more likely to proudly display these influences.

One interesting thing about the songs examined herein is that with the exception of the Offspring and U2 songs, the song in question provided the group with their breakthrough hit.

U2's "Beautiful Day" (2000)

Sounds Like

A-ha's "The Sun Always Shines on TV" (1985)

Let's remember the importance of "Beautiful Day" in U2's career. It was the featured track on their 2000 album *All That You Can't Leave Behind*. "Beautiful Day" helped drive sales of the album, thus providing U2 with a much-needed hit following the somewhat muted public response to 1997's more experimental *Pop*. The song heralded a return to U2's more familiar sound of the 1980s, a trend the band continued on their 2004 album *How to Dismantle an Atomic Bomb*. "Beautiful Day" was honored with Grammy Awards for Song of the Year and Record of the Year in 2000.

In their review of *All That You Can't Leave Behind*, Great Britain's *Q* magazine pointed out that "Beautiful Day's" chorus was strikingly similar to the chorus of A-ha's "The Sun Always Shines on TV." Specifically cited was the part of the song where Bono sings "Touch me..." and repeats the exact words and music from the A-ha song.

Shortly thereafter, U2 performed "Beautiful Day" on the MTV Europe awards show in November 2000. At the end of the song Bono sang "...and the sun always shines on TV." This was a sly admission that he was aware of the similarities between the two songs, or at least that there was a controversy about the topic.

That this was a bigger story in the UK than in the United States was probably due to the fact that "The Sun Always Shines on TV" was a No. 1 hit in the UK in 1985. Interestingly "Take on Me" was a No. 1 hit for A-ha in the United States, but failed to chart in the UK. Both songs are on the album *Hunting High and Low* which got to No. 2 in the UK largely due to the popularity of "The Sun Always Shines on TV."

Asked about the similarities between the songs, A-ha's singer and songwriter Morton Harket told a radio interviewer: "Well, it's true (the songs do sound the same). They probably wouldn't have done very well in a court case, to be honest. Bono commented once and said 'It's done out of love.' That is a comment he said out of fun. He also said 'Those guys ripped us off so many times, so we felt could get something back'…It's not entirely untrue. It's happened to some extent. But it's a blatant rip-off, basically. Still it doesn't matter. I think it was fun…and we can play 'Beautiful Day' at our gigs."[66]

Quizzed by *Q* about the similarities between the two songs, U2's guitarist Edge replied "It's positively creepy how alike they are."[67]

U2's drummer Larry Mullen told another interviewer "Yes, we noticed something was similar, but I swear it was never meant as plagiarism of anything—believe me!"[68]

U2's 2001 U.S. tour showed that they remained one of rock's most exciting live acts. "Beautiful Day" was featured on numerous U2 television appearances to promote *All That You Can't Leave Behind*. Without doubt the song had its most memorable performance at the 2002 Super Bowl. This was when the names of the September 11 victims were displayed on a giant screen during U2's performance.

In 2004 "Beautiful Day" served as the theme song of John Kerry's failed presidential campaign. In July 2005, U2 performed "Beautiful Day" during their short set at the "Live 8" concert in London's Hyde Park. Later that summer, they appeared in Oslo and sang a few lines of "The Sun Always Shines on TV" in tribute to hometown heroes A-ha.

66. Harket radio interview, "Sunday Sunset," FM 802 Japan, May 2, 2002.
67. Johnny Davis, "Fjord Fiesta!" *Q*, June 2006.
68. Ostbo Stein, "U2 With a Strong Belief in the Future." *VG*, October 7, 2002.

If A-ha is remembered at all in the United States, it is for their 1985 hit "Take on Me" and the innovative video that accompanied it. If they are seen at all, it's most likely to be on a VH1 "Where Are they Now?" segment. It's a different story in their native Norway and the rest of the world, where A-ha is still making gold albums and selling out concerts.

The Strokes's "Razorblade" (2006)

Sounds Like

Barry Manilow's "Mandy" (1975)

How bizarre is this? Obviously, these two acts are at the opposite ends of the hipness continuum. The Strokes are a press agent's dream—famous parents, celebrity girlfriends, and downtown New York attitudes—a band that might have been invented if they didn't exist already. Opinions about their music differ. Some see them as carrying on the rock and roll torch once raised by the Velvet Underground and the Rolling Stones. Others find their music exciting but highly derivative. For instance their 2001 breakthrough song "Last Night" contained allusions to both Tom Petty's "American Girl" and Iggy Pop's "Lust for Life."

"Razorblade" is on the Strokes third album, *First Impressions of Earth*. The album was highly anticipated as rock critics and fans waited to see if the band would realize their potential or reveal themselves to be mere poseurs. Many reviews of the album commented on the fact that "Razorblade" had lifted the melody of its chorus from Manilow's schmaltz classic, "Mandy." Appropriately, Manilow sings a lovelorn lyric while Strokes singer and songwriter

Julian Casablancas tells a lover that her feelings will have to take second place to his own. Strangely enough "Razorblade" manages to be a pretty good song.

Commenting on "Razorblade," Casablancas told *Spin* magazine: "We wanna sound like stuff from the future that you've never heard before while referencing stuff from the past."[69]

He later stated that "Razorblade" was one of his favorite songs on *First Impressions of Earth*.[70] Commenting on the similarities to Manilow's song, he said: "I guess I sort of knew the song ('Mandy')...I knew it but I didn't like the song so much...It's unfortunate, but yeah, what can you do?" Even though Casablancas had yet to be born when "Mandy" was a hit, the song has become a ubiquitous part of pop culture in the years since.

Manilow remains a big concert draw thirty years into a career that "Mandy" kicked off. He has fun with his image during his concerts, sometimes inquiring how many audience members were dragged to the show against their will. He recently opened a Celine Dion-style extended run show at Elvis Presley's old haunt, the Las Vegas Hilton.

69. Marc Spitz, "First Listen: The Strokes." *Spin Magazine*, July 29, 2005.
70. Evan Schlansky, "The Strokes: Hard to Explain," *American Songwriter*, March/April, 2006.

The Offspring's "Why Don't You Get a Job?" (1998)

Sounds Like

The Beatles's "Ob La Di Ob La Da" (1968)

It's hard not to like the Offspring. In the mid-1990s era of downer grunge music's radio domination, it was a pleasure to hear the Offspring's funny and somewhat goofy rock anthems like "Come out and Play" and "Self Esteem." This Orange County band brought a smile to your face while other bands were contemplating suicide in their lyrics or even committing it in real life.

That said, "Why Don't You Get a Job" is a blatant rip-off of "Ob La Di Ob La Da." Both the verses and choruses of "Why Don't You Get a Job?" are musically identical to Paul McCartney's *White Album* Beatles number. Furthermore the middle eight seems to borrow from Doris Troy's 1963 hit "Just One Look."

"Ob La Di Ob La Da" is not exactly a top-shelf Beatles product. *Abbey Road* engineer Geoff Emerick's excellent book on the Beatles,[71] makes it clear

---

71.   Geoff Emerick and Howard Massey, *Here, There, and Everywhere: My Life Recording the Beatles* (New York: Gotham, 2006).

that John Lennon despised "Ob-La-Di," while McCartney insisted on performing innumerable takes to try to get the song right—much to Lennon's displeasure. As such, "Ob-La-Di" can be seen as an encapsulation of the different musical directions Lennon and McCartney were headed by the summer of 1968. In contrast John had just completed the highly experimental sound montage, "Revolution # 9." The tensions evident during the recording of "Ob-La-Di" would soon result in the Beatles going their separate ways.

Weirdly enough McCartney was sued (unsuccessfully) by a London street singer who claimed that the Beatle had swiped the song's lyrics from him.

The White Stripes's "Fell in Love with a Girl" (2001)

Sounds Like

The Pretenders's "Middle of the Road" (1983)

"Fell in Love with a Girl" had an artsy video that helped the White Stripes go from cult status to full-fledged rock stars. The song also had a chorus that was obviously influenced by the Pretenders's "Middle of the Road."

"Fell in Love with a Girl" is a great song. It's stripped-down slice of ballsy rock and roll that was much welcomed after the long, dark night of '90s grunge.

The Stripes have proven themselves to be more that a one-hit wonder, but they will always be a bit indebted to the Pretenders's Chrissie Hynde for providing the chorus of the song that put them on the map.

In 2006 White formed a new group called the Raconteurs. The band's first single, "Steady, as She Goes," had a guitar riff and rhythm that was an obvious lift from Joe Jackson's "Is She Really Going Out With Him?"

Radiohead's "Creep" (1993)

Sounds Like

The Hollies's "The Air That I Breathe" (1974)

The British band Radiohead is arguably the most successful rock group—both artistically and commercially—working today. Their 1993 breakthrough hit "Creep" has become a modern rock classic. "Creep" features a soaring chorus that belies the song's disaffected lyric. Considering Radiohead's ultra-hip credentials, it's shocking to learn that co-authorship of the song is now credited to Albert Hammond. Yes, the same Albert Hammond who sang "It Never Rains in California" back in 1972.

How did this happen? Hammond is the co-author of the 1974 Hollies hit "The Air That I Breathe," a slow, dreamy song later used to great effect in the movie the *Virgin Suicides*. Radiohead used the chord pattern of "The Air That I Breathe" to create the slow verses of "Creep." Those verses beautifully set up the crescendo of "Creep's" chorus.

Now there's nothing wrong with copying a chord pattern, but "Creep" goes on to directly copy from the melody line of "The Air That I Breathe" during a brief bridge section following the second chorus. It was this section that caused the publishers of "The Air That I Breathe" to bring a lawsuit against Radiohead. According to Hammond's Web site (www.alberthammond.com),

Thom Yorke and Radiohead agreed that "Creep" was partially based on "The Air That I Breathe." A settlement was agreed to that gave Hammond and his partner a writing credit on "Creep" and a portion of the song's royalties. Hammond now claims authorship on one of the corniest and on one of the hippest songs in rock history.

With the settlement complete, Hammond professed to be complimented that a group of Radiohead's stature had been inspired by his song.

Franz Ferdinand's "Take Me Out" (2004)

Sounds Like

Ringo Starr's "Back off Boogaloo" (1971)

Scotland's Franz Ferdinand became rock's flavor of the month in 2004 with their hit song "Take Me Out." Its popularity was helped by the dearth of decent rock songs on the radio at the time, and by listeners' hunger for anything approaching a decent song.

The song was musically similar to Ringo Starr's early solo hit, "Back Off Boogaloo." This fact was pointed out by ex-Libertines/current Babyshambles singer Pete Doherty in 2005 when he said that in his opinion, "Take Me Out" was a rip-off of "Back Off Boogaloo."

Ringo surprised everybody when he had the most solo success of any of his fellow Beatles in the years immediately after the group's 1970 demise. "Back off Boogaloo" has been a staple of Ringo's *All Star* shows since he began touring regularly in 1989. Curiously the song has been mostly absent from U.S. oldies radio through the years.

Strangely enough Modest Mouse's 2004 hit "Float On" seems to have taken some of its inspiration from the guitar riff in "Take Me Out."

The Flaming Lips's "Fight Test" (2002)

Sounds Like

Cat Stevens's "Father and Son" (1970)

Cat Stevens is the guy who threw it all away. Turning his back on rock superstardom, he changed his name to Yusuf Islam the late '70s and has lived as a devout Muslim ever since. His beliefs are such that making music with instruments is frowned upon. Thus his few performances or recordings usually featured vocals only.

"Father and Son" is one of the more popular Cat Stevens recordings, a song well known to anyone who grew up with FM radio.

The Flaming Lips have been making records for over twenty years. Their career path tells the admirable tale of a band that has put creativity ahead of the concerns of the market. They are today's inheritors of the 1960s spirit of psychedelic experimentation. "Fight Test" is the first song on their 2002 CD *Yoshimi Battles the Pink Robots*, an album that was something of a breakthrough for the Lips. The song bears a close musical similarity to "Father and Son," so much so that Stevens's publishers forced the Lips publisher to split all songwriting royalties on "Fight Test."

Flaming Lips's singer and songwriter Wayne Coyne discussed the issue in depth with *Undercover* magazine: "I knew from the get go that there were some similarities. We actually changed it while we were making the song. That's where I made the mistake. If you have a song that you think sounds like another song you should contact the publishing company and say "I have a song here, let's cut a deal that lets everyone walk away feeling good." Because I didn't do that and it was released there was no leg for me to stand on. I wished I had done it in a different way."[72]

Coyne refers to preemptive agreements such as those the Rolling Stones and R.E.M. reached with publishers prior to the release of "Anybody Seen My Baby" and "Hope" respectively.

In 2003 "Fight Test" provided the ironic title track to the Flaming Lips EP of cover songs which included their bizarre version of Kylie Minogue's "Can't Get it Out of My Head."

In early 2006 reports stated that Islam was at work on his first secular album since 1978's *Back to Earth.*[73]

---

72.   Paul Cashmere, "Flaming Lips Interview." *Undercover Magazine.*

73.   Melinda Newman, *Billboard Magazine,* "Yusuf Islam Readying New Pop Album," March 17, 2006.

X

Case History
Bolton vs. Isley

Michael Bolton's "Love is a Wonderful Thing" (1991)

Sounds Like

The Isley Brothers's "Love is a Wonderful Thing" (1966)

In this chapter we'll take a closer look at some of the legal issues involved in pursuing a copyright infringement case. These issues, namely the questions of accessibility and substantial similarity, pertain to all cases where U.S. copyright infringement is claimed. But more importantly, it gives us a chance to goof on Michael Bolton. Or does it?

Background[74]
Bolton's song, "Love is a Wonderful Thing," was a No. 4 Billboard hit in April 1991. It was the first single released from his album, *Time, Love and Tenderness*. The album went on to sell more than ten million copies worldwide.

---

74.   Trial summary 12/00. "Michael Bolton and Subconscious Plagiarism."
      IP Issues.

In January 1992, Bolton and songwriting partner Andy Goldmark were sued by the Isley Brothers who claimed that "Love is a Wonderful Thing" plagiarized their 1966 song of the same name. The case went before a jury in early 1994.

The Issue of Accessibility

A plaintiff in a copyright infringement case must prove that the accused had access to the song they are accused of copying. For this reason, most recording artists will not listen to unsolicited tapes sent to them by aspiring songwriters, lest they later be sued by someone who could legitimately claim that they had access to the songwriter's material. By doing this, an artist is erecting a wall of inaccessibility around himself.

The Isleys's lawyers had their work cut out for them because the group's "Love Is a Wonderful Thing" was a very obscure recording. United Artists released the song in 1966. It had been copyrighted and recorded by the Isleys (Ronald, Rudolph, and O'Kelly) in 1964. (Ronald would testify that the band's guitarist, a certain Jimi Hendrix, had helped him compose the song.) In the meantime, the Isleys had recorded several hits after moving to Motown Records in 1965. These included the classic, "This Old Heart of Mine." The 1966 release of a two-year-old recording was an attempt to cash in on the success of "This Old Heart of Mine." Unfortunately "Love Is a Wonderful Thing" was not a hit, failing make any of the Top 100 charts at the time. The closest it came was a No. 110 ranking on Billboard's Bubbling Under chart. The song was released only as a 45, and did not appear on any Isley Brothers album until 1991.

Bolton claimed he had never heard the Isleys's song. That made the accessibility issue paramount. This made the case different in character from the "My Sweet Lord" case wherein George Harrison freely admitted to having heard "She's So Fine," a No. 1 hit.

The Isleys's lawyers presented four arguments in seeking to prove that Bolton and Goldmark could have heard the Isleys's "Love is a Wonderful Thing:"

1. In 1966, as teenagers living in Connecticut, Bolton and Goldmark admitted that they listened to a lot of R & B music. Bolton sang in a band that did covers of soul-music hits and admitted that his brother "had a pretty good record collection."

2. Three DJs testified that they had played the Isleys's song on radio stations in various cities, including New York, during 1966. Jerry Blavat

said he played "Love is Wonderful Thing" five times during the three-month run of the TV show *The Discophonic Scene,* which he said aired in New York and (possibly) New Haven, where Bolton then lived. The two other DJs cited stations still playing the song in 1994.

3. Bolton had admitted to being a big Isley Brothers's fan. Ronnie Isley testified that upon meeting Bolton in 1988, Bolton said, "I know this guy…I have all his stuff…I know everything he's done."

4. A work tape of Bolton and Goldmark composing their song recorded Bolton inquiring if the song they were working on was Marvin Gaye's "Some Kind of Wonderful." The Isleys's lawyers contended that Bolton was actually referring to the Isleys's song, but had confused it with Gaye's.

Now it was Bolton's turn. He claimed that he couldn't have copied the Isleys's song because he had never heard it. Three R & B experts, one of which was Motown songwriter Lamont Dozier, testified that they had never heard the Isleys's "Love is a Wonderful Thing." In his own testimony, Bolton made these points:

1. The work tape actually proved that he and Goldmark had composed their song themselves.

2. One hundred twenty-nine songs with the title "Love is a Wonderful Thing" have been registered with the U.S. Office of Copyrights. Eighty-four of them were registered prior to 1964. This point made was that just because a song had that title did not prove that the composer had heard the Isleys's song.

3. *TV Guides* from 1966 did not list "The Discophonic Scene" as having been televised in Connecticut.

"Substantial Similarity"

In addition to proving access, the plaintiff must also prove that the song in question exhibits "substantial similarity." This concept consists of a two-part test: *ex*trinsic similarity and *in*trinsic similarity. The first requires an objective approach wherein experts testify and dissect the songs musically. Determining intrinsic similarity is more subjective and asks "whether the ordinary, reasonable person would find the total concept and feel of the works to be substantially similar." It kind of reminds you of former Supreme Court Justice Potter

Stewart's "I-know-it–when-I-see-it" standard for determining what constitutes obscenity, doesn't it?

In attempting to prove extrinsic similarity, the Isley side called musicologist Dr. Gerald Eskelin. He pointed out five points of musical similarity between the two songs: the title hook phrase (including the lyric, rhythm and pitch), the shifted cadence, the instrumental figures, the verse/chorus relationship, and the fade ending. Bolton's expert disputed these claims.

The Decision

The jury ruled in favor of the Isleys. They agreed that Bolton had had reasonable access to the song and that the two songs were both intrinsically and extrinsically similar. In a separate phase of the trial, the jury decided that sixty-six percent of the profits of the Bolton song derived from elements infringed from the Isleys's song. In addition, they found that twenty-eight percent of the profits from the album *Time, Love and Tenderness* resulted from the fact that the song, "Love Is a Wonderful Thing," was on it. This meant Sony had to pay $4.2 million, Bolton $932,924, Goldmark $220,785, and their music publishers $75,900.

The Ninth Court of Appeals affirmed this ruling and award in May 2000. This was in spite of the fact that they seemed sympathetic to Bolton's argument regarding access. The court went as far as to state "This may be a weak case of access and a circumstantial case of substantial similarity…" The ruling went on to state that just because the Isleys had a weak case regarding access, it did not mean that songs needed a higher degree of similarity to make up for it. (The opposite does hold true, however. A very strong access case lowers the need for proving a strong substantial similarity case. This is the inverse ratio rule.) The Court found that Bolton had subconsciously copied the Isleys's song. In January 2001, the U.S. Supreme Court refused to hear Bolton's appeal.[75]

In February 2001, Ronald Isley's assets were purchased by the Pullman Group as part of his bankruptcy proceeding. Among those filing unsuccessful bids was Michael Bolton. Had he been successful, he would have owned Ronald Isley's stake in the original "Love is a Wonderful Thing."

---

75.   Emily Farache, "Supreme Court Smacks Down Michael Bolton," *E News Online*, January 22, 2001.

In October 2005, Ronald Isley was convicted of income tax evasion. In September, 2006 he was sentenced to thirty-seven months in prison.

Conclusion

It hurts to say it, but I think Bolton got shafted in this case. Even finding a copy of the Isleys's recording of "Love is a Wonderful Thing" is quite a task. The only CD or LP on which it appears is 1991's *Complete UA Sessions*. To my ears the songs don't sound all that alike save for the title and Bolton's attempt to recreate a Motown feel. The Isleys's song is much faster and differs melodically from Bolton's song.

Since the evidence against Bolton proves pretty flimsy to my ears (I found little intrinsic similarity), and to the Court of Appeals as well, I'm left to wonder what role Bolton's somewhat dubious public persona played in these proceedings.

XI

Musical Family Trees

Musical Family Tree I

Chuck Berry's "Too Much Monkey Business" (1957)

Bob Dylan's "Subterranean Homesick Blues" (1965)

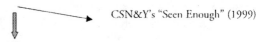 CSN&Y's "Seen Enough" (1999)

R.E.M.'s "It's the End of the World As We Know It (And I Feel Fine)" (1987)

Looking back on the rock and roll pioneers of the 1950s, it is now apparent the one who has been the most influential in a musical sense is the man from St. Louis, Chuck Berry. While it was Elvis Presley who became a cultural icon, Berry's early hits such as "Roll Over, Beethoven" and "Johnny B. Goode" were the foundation upon which the rock and roll of the '60s and '70s was built. His songwriting skills are sometimes undervalued because they usually didn't deal with heavy subject matter. A closer look reveals Berry to be a very clever lyricist with a gift for making up words of his own, eg, "motorvating."

Rock critic Robert Christgau once wrote that Berry was "the man who taught George Harrison and Keith Richards to play guitar."[76] Indeed, looking back on the psychedelic era of the late 1960s, Richards once stated that it initially filled him with trepidation because all he really knew how to do was to play Chuck Berry riffs on guitar.

Perhaps less well known is Berry's influence on the most influential performer of the 1960s, Bob Dylan. Included on Dylan's highly influential *Bringing It All Back Home* album, "Subterranean Homesick Blues" was among Dylan's earliest recorded attempts at rock and roll; it was also highly indebted to "Too Much Monkey Business" both musically and for its laundry-list approach to the lyrics. Dylan confirmed this in his *Biography* liner notes.

R.E.M. recorded a souped-up version of "Subterranean," in "It's the End of the World As We Know It (And I Feel Fine)." They retained the musical feel and lyrical-free association of Dylan's song, then added a rip-roaring chorus all their own.

For those of you who are thinking Billy Joel's 1989 No. 1 hit, "We Didn't Start the Fire," should have been included here, I would say you're half right. While lyrically it was a direct descendent of the above songs, at least the "Piano Man" came up with something of an original melody.

Alas the same cannot be said of "Seen Enough," a Stephen Stills song on the 1999 Crosby, Stills, Nash & Young album *Looking Forward*. Its similarity to "Subterranean Homesick Blues" earned Dylan a co-writing credit after the song had been completed.

Striking images permeate every line of "Subterranean Homesick Blues." With few exceptions, this kind of lyrical poetry has been sadly lacking in rock for many years.

---

76. Jim Miller, Editor. *The Rolling Stone Illustrated History of Rock 'n' Roll.* New York: Random House, 1980, 56.

Musical Family Tree II

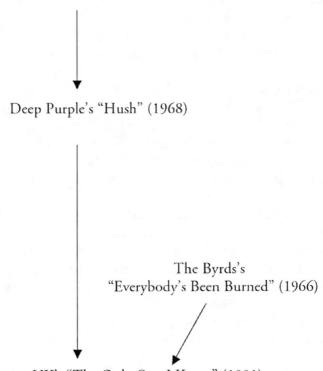

The Beatles's "A Day in the Life" (1967)

Deep Purple's "Hush" (1968)

The Byrds's
"Everybody's Been Burned" (1966)

The Charlatans UK's "The Only One I Know" (1991)

I suppose we should start at the top. "A Day in the Life's" wordless midsection sung by John Lennon (coming right after the section McCartney sang) appears to have inspired the chorus of "Hush." In "Hush" the melody was again sung but had no words. It instead consisted of "las" instead of the "ahs" of "A Day in the Life." "Hush" was distinctive for its rumbling rhythm and Jon Lord's electric organ. The song was written by American songwriter Joe South of "Games People Play" fame. It was originally recorded in late 1967 by Billy Joe Royal of "Down in the Boondocks" fame. Royal's version of "Hush" did not gain much fame, failing to dent the Top 40. In addition to "Boondocks," South also composed Royal's lost classic, "I Knew You When," and Lynn Anderson's "Rose Garden."

Deep Purple's recording of "Hush" went to No. 4 on U.S. charts. It kicked off a career that saw the Purps become one of rock's most successful early-'70s bands.

The Charlatans (the "UK" was added later for legal reasons) came out of the late-'80s Manchester, England, music scene that also included the Stone Roses and the Happy Mondays. They have outlasted those groups and persevered through many crises, including a nervous breakdown and the 1996 death of keyboardist Rob Collins. Their 1999 album, *Us & Only Us*, contained some of their best work ever. They remain more popular in Europe than in the United States.

The Charlatans UK directly copied "Hush's" rhythm for "The Only One I Know." The prominent Hammond organ was also reminiscent of Deep Purple's "Hush." Perhaps when coming up with a middle eight for the song they figured they might as well steal that, too. They did just that when they blatantly copied the words and music of David Crosby's excellent Byrds's song "Everybody's Been Burned."

Congratulations, Charlatans UK. Most of the artists mentioned in this book were content to rip off one song at a time, but you ripped off two…Or was it three?

AND FURTHERMORE…Perhaps inspired by "The Only One I Love," Kula Shaker (remember them?) recorded a cover of "Hush" in 1996.

Musical Family Tree III

Solomon Linda and the Evening Birds's "Mbube" (1939)

The Weavers's "Wimoweh" (1952)

The Tokens's "The Lion Sleeps Tonight" (1961)

Thirty-five years before being introduced to Paul Simon's *Graceland* album, Americans got a taste of South African Zulu music on the Weavers's recording of "Wimoweh." Group member Pete Seeger had discovered the song amongst a pile of imported 78s a friend had given him, and he knew the song would fit well into the Weavers's folk repertoire. The Weavers's spirited recording of "Mbube,"[77] retitled "Wimoweh," was fairly faithful to the original, and rose to No. 6 on the U.S. charts in 1952. The song was credited to "Paul Campbell," a pseudonym for the Weavers and their management. Claiming publishing on songs that were in the public domain was a widespread practice at the time. Unfortunately for the Weavers, they were about to see their careers virtually destroyed when Seeger and two fellow Weavers were identified as Communists in testimony before the House Un-American Activities Committee (HUAC). Unfortunately for Solomon Linda, the man who had composed "Mbube," (Zulu for "the lion"), the music publishing industry would do precious little to compensate him for composing a song that would become one of the biggest hits of the rock era.

Linda had not even written down the music at the time he recorded it, so publishing royalties were not exactly foremost in his mind. In fact the whole concept of copyrights was nonexistent in South Africa at the time. Artists were paid for performing on a session and that was the end of it. The recording took place in Johannesburg in what was the only recording studio in sub-Saharan Africa at that time. Records of "Mbube" were pressed for sale in the black townships of apartheid South Africa. By the end of the 1940s it was reckoned to have sold over 100,000 copies. The monies earned by the record did not go to Linda but to the owner of his record company, Eric Gallo.

When "Wimoweh" became a hit for the Weavers, Gallo registered a U.S. copyright on "Mbube." Then he made a rather foolish deal with the Weavers's publishers, the Richmond Organization (TRO). He offered to give them the rights to "Mbube" in exchange for the right to administer the publishing on "Wimoweh" in certain African countries.

Gallo did nothing to protect Linda's interests. Seeger recognized Linda as the true author of "Wimoweh," and later claimed that he sought to compensate him. Seeger claimed that he sent Linda a check for one thousand dollars

---

77. Historical background based on "75 Years of Gallo Music." *Sunday Times (South Africa)*, September 23, 2001, and Malan, Rian; May 25, 2000, "In the Jungle." *Rolling Stone.*

and said claimed he asked TRO to send future royalties to Linda. It appears that little or no money from TRO ever got to Linda or his family.

While the Weavers's career had been derailed, "Wimoweh" was only gaining popularity. It was recorded by band leader Jimmy Dorsey and included on the Kingston Trio's massively popular LP, *Live at the Hungry I,* an album that sold well enough to remain on the charts for over three years in the late 1950s.

The Tokens were a vocal group from New York. They were familiar with the Weavers's "Wimoweh" and had sung their version of the song for their producers, Hugo Perretti and Luigi Creatore. ("Huge and Luge" were cousins and very successful producers who worked with Sam Cooke, among many others.) Unsatisfied, the producers turned to songwriter George Weiss to polish the thing up. Weiss had just authored Elvis Presley's smash "Can't Help Falling in Love" and came back with "The Lion Sleeps Tonight," applying lyrics to the wordless melody of "Mbube." To be fair, Weiss, Creatore, Perretti, and the Tokens came up with an awesome production, a song that stayed at No. 1 on the Billboard chart for three weeks and has been heard on oldies radio for the past forty years. The Tokens later claimed that Weiss had appropriated their ideas for the song and claimed them as his own.

No fools themselves, Perretti and Creatore knew that "Paul Campbell" was a jive creation to claim credit on a song in the public domain. Thus "The Lion Sleeps Tonight" was initially credited to "Perretti-Creatore-Weiss." Outraged that someone would steal a song that he had already successfully stolen, TRO got his lawyers to inform Perretti, Creatore, and Weiss that "Mbube" was NOT in the public domain, but was a copyrighted work that he owned. But why let legal technicalities get in way of a making a great deal of money? A deal was struck wherein TRO would get a one-half publishers' share and Perretti, Creatore and Weiss would get the other half with writers' credits.

"The Lion Sleeps Tonight" was a smash. It was a record that sounded like nothing else on the radio at the time. Brian Wilson was reportedly so blown away by the song that he pulled his car off the road to listen the first time he heard it. The Tokens's song stayed atop the Billboard chart for three weeks, and also hit No. 1 in many other nations including Britain, where a cover version by the Karl Denver Trio was a No. 1 hit.

Solomon Linda died in 1962, shortly after seeing his creation become an international success. Although he received scant financial rewards for creating "Wimoweh" and most of "The Lion Sleeps Tonight," he was still an acclaimed figure among the Zulu people. Years later his daughter Fildah remembered that her father was "happy" when "The Lion Sleeps Tonight" became a worldwide smash. "He didn't know he was supposed to get something."

Ensuing years saw the publishing royalties for "The Lion Sleeps Tonight" continue to grow. A carbon copy of the Tokens recording by Robert John became a No. 3 hit in the United States 1972. In 1994 the song was included in Disney's *Lion King* film and soundtrack. Some money made it back to the Linda family over the years, but it was but a small percentage of what Linda and his heirs would have been entitled to had a copyright been registered and enforced from the beginning.

1989 saw the absurd spectacle of both sets of copyright claimants: the Richmond Organization and Weiss, Creatore, and Peretti threatening to sue each other over the authorship of a song none of the principals had originally created. To make a long story short, it was decreed that Weiss and company would gain full ownership of the song, with ten percent of the royalties to go to the Linda family. An extensive investigation by reporter Rian Malan found that under this new arrangement, only about twelve thousand dollars had made it back to the family during the '90s. The '90s were a period in which "The Lion Sleeps Tonight" was included on the *Lion King* album and had numerous additional cover versions. Therefore, the twelve-thousand-dollar figure seems low.

In early 2006, legal efforts on behalf of the Linda family had finally resulted in what the family viewed as an equitable settlement.[78] Their cause had been championed in the South African media by Malan and others.

Also in 2006, Ladysmith Black Mambazo recorded "Mbube" with Taj Mahal guesting on their album *Long Walk to Freedom*. Speaking about the history of "Mbube" and "The Lion Sleeps Tonight" Mahal told the BBC/PRI radio program *The World*: "I personally believe that the whole music industry is built on the backs of being able to take music from people who are unable to protect themselves...I mean flat out steal."[79]

What you take away from this story may depend on what perspective you view it from. To the modern observer in the West, it appears to be a case of slick businessmen exploiting the art and people of a less-developed culture. Malan reached a somewhat different conclusion. He notes that Linda never

---

78.   Sharon LaFraniere, "In the Jungle, the Unjust Jungle, a Small Victory." *New York Times*, March 22, 2006.

79.   Marco Werman; Corespondent, *PRI: The World*, "Global Hit." February 28, 2006.

expected to make riches from his music and took pleasure in knowing that it had become world famous. He was a popular live performer among the Zulu people, and the style of music he performed is known today as Mbube, after his song. Malan concluded that Linda had achieved greatly given the circumstances of living in that place and time—apartheid South Africa in the mid-twentieth century.

Afterword

Have pity on the poor songwriter. Consider the difficulty of his or her task—to create a melody that is both familiar and yet new and original. This is a task akin to the dilemma of the baseball pitcher whose manager visits the mound and advises, "Don't give him anything good to hit, but don't walk him, either."

Many of the writers discussed herein drifted a bit too far into familiar territory. It's interesting and possibly instructive that we find so many of the songs that were "borrowed" from earlier tunes ended up giving the borrower their first hit and a toe-hold in the extremely competitive music business. This may indicate a successful strategy for getting noticed in a crowded field. It's for this reason that A and R people often advise new bands to record cover songs of previous hits.

It's worth noting that when Paul McCartney first came up with the melody to "Yesterday," he said that for weeks he went around humming the melody to friends, asking them to identify what song it was from.[80] He wanted to be sure that he was not claiming someone else's song as his own. Many other artists I've covered could have avoided a lot of headaches had they exercised the same due diligence that McCartney did, at least in this instance.

In the spring of 2006, Bob Dylan began a show on XM Satellite Radio in which he acts as a DJ and plays some of his favorite music. Many commenta-

---

80. Authors Spencer Leigh and Alan Clayson made news when he claimed that the melody McCartney had in mind was "Answer Me, My Love," a Nat King Cole hit. While I would have been happy to include this item in this book, I don't think the claim is justified because I don't think the songs sound that much alike. Listen for yourself and see what you think. (See: Leigh and Clayson. *The Walrus Was Paul: 101 Beatles Myths Debunked.* Surrey. U.K.: Chrome Dreams, 2004.)

tors have expressed surprise at the broad range of musical taste that he exhibited. Dylan played music by Frank Sinatra, Merle Haggard, Jimi Hendrix, Muddy Waters, Judy Garland, and even L.L. Cool J's "Mama Said Knock You Out." And that was just in the first two weeks.

After reading this book I hope you won't be surprised when you read such stories about great songwriters.

Someone once said that if you want to become an expert on a subject, write a book about it. I don't know about the expert part, but writing this book has been a wonderful journey on which I've discovered artists who I was previously unaware of. Thanks for sharing the journey—I can only hope that you enjoyed it as much as I did.

Bibliography

Whitburn, Joel. *The Billboard Book of Top 40 Hits.* New York: Billboard Books, 1996.

Strong, Martin C. *The Great Rock Discography, Fifth Edition.* Edinburgh: Mojo Books, 2006.

Erlewine, Woodstra, and Bogdanov. *All Music Guide.* San Francisco: Miller Freeman, 1994.

About the Author

Tim English has written about rock music for nearly thirty years. *Sounds Like Teen Spirit* is the product of many years of listening and research. Mr. English lives in New Jersey with his wife and daughter. His work has appeared in *Upstage Magazine*, which provides first rate coverage of the music scene in metro New York and New Jersey.

978-0-595-39619-1
0-595-39619-4

Printed in the United States
65416LVS00008B/211-222

9 780595 396191